EVERYDAY MATTERS

EVERYDAY MATTERS

By
Elise Seyfried

*To Judy,
Blessings, everyday!*

Copyright ©2015 by Elise Seyfried

All rights reserved. No part of this book may be reproduced, stored, or transmitted by any means—whether auditory, graphic, mechanical or electronic—without written permission of both publisher and author, except in the case of brief excerpts used in critical articles and reviews. Unauthorized reproduction of any part of this work is illegal and is punishable by law.

ISBN 978-1-329-02201-0

Scripture quotations are from New Revised Standard Version Bible, copyright ©1989 by the National Council of the Churches of Christ in the United States of America. Used by permission. All rights reserved.

Many of these articles originally appeared in the *Chestnut Hill Local.*

INTRODUCTION

Everyday Matters: things that happen in the course of one's daily life.

Everyday Matters: one's daily life does matter

Take #3!

It has been five years since my first book of essays, *Unhaling*, was published, and almost four since *Underway*. While much has changed (I now have a wonderful daughter-in-law and very precious baby grandson; my youngest is in college; everyone is busily building grown up lives for themselves), some things never have. I am still disorganized and nervous and fearful a lot of the time. I'm still a superstitious procrastinator who can't watch sports or play card games to save her soul, who does a lousy job of keeping up her house and her appearance. I still stumble through life, always meaning well but making mistakes all over the place. Amazingly, though, God hasn't given up on me yet, and I truly believe He never will.

So here we go with another collection of musings about my "everydays." My days include my continuing work as Spiritual Formation director at a Lutheran church and a freelance writer, and the challenges of being a wife, mother, and now a Nana as well. The cover features a Celtic cross, because, in Celtic spirituality, everything we do is sacred. Washing dishes, doing the laundry, driving the car...all are infused with the Spirit of God. And it's a darned good thing, because God's spirit is what I need to get me through breaking the dishes, shrinking the laundry, denting the car. It is my hope that reading these stories will get you thinking about YOUR "everydays" and the amazing grace contained within them.

All my love and thanks to the remarkable people in my life, my family and friends. My time with you is a joy, and the inspiration for my writing.

Contents

A RIDE ON THE MIRACLE-ROUND 1
FRAIDY CAT 5
ARE YOU THERE, ELISE? IT'S ME, GOD 9
MASTER OF THE UNIVERSE 13
GROWING, GROWING, GONE 15
FELLOW TRAVELERS 17
A MATTER OF TRUST 19
TAKE A NUMBER 23
WHERE TO? 27
DON'T PLAY GAMES WITH ME! 31
MY MOUTH DROPS CLOSED 35
DIAL TONE 39
…BUT FOR THE GRACE OF GOD 43
B–E–DOUBLE R – I – G – A – N SPELLS BERRIGAN 45
FOR ALL THE SAINTS 49
I'M GONNA MAKE YOU LOVE ME 53
QUITTING TIME 57
STUCK ON YOU 61
THE KEY 65
THIS OLD HOUSE 69
STRANGER THAN FICTION 73
THE BEST BIRTHDAY EVER 75
PHOTO OP 79

DO I HEAR A WALTZ?	83
PROCRASTI-NATION	85
FOR SALE	89
BUSTING OUT ALL OVER	91
THE MAGIC PASSPORT	95
WONDERS NEVER CEASE	99
WAITING FOR GODOT IN LOGAN SQUARE	103
OF A CERTAIN AGE	107
NO MORE TEARS	111
HOME, SWEET HOMESCHOOL	113
LIFE WITH STEVO	117
DREAM A LITTLE DREAM	121
LEGACY	125
LET THE GAMES BEGIN	127
ACCENTUATING IT	129
SPORTS NUT (NOT)	133
FAKING IT	137
THE PLEASURE OF THEIR COMPANY	139
NEVER TOO LATE	143
ANGELS AMONG US	145
ZEN AND THE ART OF BABY HOLDING	147
SAVE THE DATE!	149

A RIDE ON THE MIRACLE-ROUND

"Mommy, you know the ninja turtles came first. Then came the time of the dinosaur, then pirates, then people!"

--Evan Seyfried, age 4

Most of the time, I am perfectly content to have children who are in their late teens and twenties. They can be trusted (usually) with full glasses of milk, they don't cry when it's time for bed, they no longer leave 3,000,000 Lego blocks scattered across the floor (and yes, stepping barefoot on a Lego in the dark hurts like heck). We can take a trip with them without renting a U-Haul for the crib, highchair, playpen and jolly jumper. So life with our offspring is good, all in all. And yet...

I miss my babies. I miss my toddlers. I miss the silly and lovable things they'd say, SO much. I remember when my journal-keeping petered out for each of them, around age eight or so. One day one of the kids asked me why I stopped writing, and I said (only half-kiddingly), "I stopped writing when you stopped being cute."

I actually remember when I stopped being cute. I had been a rather precocious child, given to putting on one-person reenactments of the <u>entire</u> Sound of Music at my Nana's cocktail parties. Well, Nana thought I was cute anyway, even as her beleaguered guests gripped their highballs and gritted their teeth while I warbled on and on about how to solve a problem like Maria. One time when I was around five, I was REALLY naughty. When Mom sent me to my room, I hotly defended myself: "You can't punish me. I don't know any better. I haven't reached the age of reason yet!" Anyway, there came a day when my *mots* were suddenly not so *bon*, when my utterances didn't elicit a chuckle from the grownups anymore. More than many other milestones on the road to adulthood, that one hurt.

Don't know if my kids recall a similar defining moment when they left the land of sunshine and butterflies that is early childhood—or how much of that enchanted idyll they remember at all. Thanks to the journals, I can relive those days anytime I want. Sorry to brag, but I think the little Seyfrieds were pretty cute.

Months after young Rose saw a picture in the Bible of the Holy Spirit descending in the form of a dove, she observed seagulls at the beach: "Look at all those Holy Spirits!" PJ at age three memorized the entire script of *Aladdin* along with me (and unbeknownst to me). As I crammed for opening night at the children's theatre, suddenly a tiny voice behind my chair piped up, "Hi dare! I'm your genie!" Evan mastered a bizarre but hilarious facial expression that came to be known, simply, as The Look. The Look featured eyes rolled upwards, mouth turned comically down. We have photos of The Look buried in the sand, The Look going out to sea, The Look at dinner, at the zoo, at Christmas. Sheridan rode the "miracle-round" at Funland, while small Julie would greet me on cold winter mornings with "Good morna, Mommy. You got your robot (robe) on!"

And I'm sure that any of you who are parents could top my tales. I'm equally sure that you yourselves (trust me!) were at least as precious as my babies, back in the day. Kids, every one of them, say and do the darnedest things. And they give us the greatest of gifts—joy and laughter.

Our days of "cute" seem to be numbered for sure. We grow taller, we master language, we become self-conscious. But what if we kept looking at the world through child-colored glasses? What if we continued to play with words and concepts, use our imaginations to transport us to wondrous places? That's what artists do, and scientists too. But really, anyone can do it—from the truck driver to the carpenter to the nurse. It's a matter of finding the amazing in the everyday, finding the special that's hidden in the mundane. For some people it takes a crisis, like a serious illness, to bring them back to just cherishing existence itself. But too often, the toddler with his happy plunge into each glorious day disappears when the spelling tests and braces and inhibitions arrive—sadly, never to return.

Today's challenge, then: get back in touch with your "cute." That adorable little person, believe it or not, is still in there. Try to imagine yourself as God sees you. God enjoys you, and wants you to enjoy yourself and your world. Laugh, and make others laugh too, whenever you can.

So, go on, take a wild and wonderful ride on the miracle-round that is life. And may all your seagulls be Holy Spirits.

FRAIDY CAT

"Do not fear, for I am with you; I will bring your offspring from the east, and from the west I will gather you."

--Isaiah 43:5

To say I am easily spooked, would be like saying Itzhak Perlman plays little violin ditties well: the understatement of the century. I never progressed beyond age five in the bravery department. My one and only horror movie, *The Exorcist*, was attended just because I was dating my husband Steve—a crowd was going to the midnight show and I didn't want to wimp out. Luckily, in the darkness, no one could tell my eyes were shut and my ears plugged.

When I was a new driver, I crept hesitantly out into the traffic, cringing at the thought of an imminent crash. Horns tooting behind me, I maintained a snappy 35 mph on the expressway and still felt imperiled. Mind you, I've never had an accident, and my only ticket was the result of parking on the wrong side of the road during a street cleaning. But I'm due for a disaster, wouldn't you think? So I venture out to Shop' N Bag for groceries in the rain, muttering "Hail Marys" under my breath, the very model of how NOT to operate a motor vehicle.

As you can imagine, I made the ideal parent. Every stomach bug was the plague, every fever, meningitis. When baby Sheridan slept too little, Evan too much, Rosie not at all; when toddler PJ chose screaming over speaking, and newborn Julie failed to respond to sound as much as I felt she should, something was always capital W Wrong. I'm surprised our pediatrician Dr. Lockman didn't add a nuisance charge to the Seyfried bill for all my extra calls and questions over the years.

The kids' teens gave me ample opportunities to be fearful. Sheridan, at 18, moved downtown to an apartment, solo (the Curtis Institute of Music did not have dorms). I tried not to think of the danger he undoubtedly put himself in, but thought of little else. One night, late, he called to "chat." I enjoyed our phone visit at first. When conversational topics ran out, and we were looping back to The Weather, Take Two, and still he talked...something was capital W Wrong! Finally, he said, "I just turned my key in the lock, Mom, I'm home. There were two weird guys walking behind me all the way from the train station, and I felt safer talking to you." "Oh, honey..." I began, horrified. "OK bye," he hung up, next stop Dreamland. I, of course, was awake all night.

When Rosie went to Thailand as a high school junior, my fears for her general well-being were legion. Rose tried to calm me with her description of Chiang Rai as totally safe, and the Thai people as gentle and completely non-violent—but I wasn't buying it. When she didn't dial in on time for our infrequent Skype sessions, I instantly imagined her held for ransom somewhere, or under a mosquito net sweltering with malaria. Rosie came home at last, with nothing but the most wonderful stories of her year in Asia—gorgeous scenery, fabulous food, friends for life.

You'd think after that, I might lighten up a tad when she decided on college in Boston. Not a chance. Just before her departure, I sought out mace or something similar. I was surprised to find that the likeliest local spot to purchase was a nearby gun shop. I darted in, looking quite the opposite of a seasoned firearms buff, and asked the clerk if the store carried pepper spray. His immediate response? "Where is your daughter going to college?" Wow, how did he know?

Needless to say, I don't think Rosie carried the pepper spray once. She has never agreed with my vision of the world as a Dark and Frightening Place—and neither have the other kids.

That bad things happen in this world, no one can dispute. But simple common sense can go a long way towards protecting us from trouble. And when trouble comes along anyway, despite our best efforts, we can either quake in fear or face our fortune bravely. Some of the most challenged folks I know have the most upbeat and optimistic points of view. Meanwhile I, a lucky duck by any standard, lie in bed and dread the unknowns of each new dawn.

How much of life is perception? Why is my perception so often skewed in a negative direction?

When, oh Lord, will I stop being so scared?

ARE YOU THERE, ELISE? IT'S ME, GOD

"But the Lord answered her, "Martha, Martha, you are worried and distracted by many things; there is need of only one thing..."
--Luke 10:41-42

Among the Commandments I break with regularity, #3 is a weekly offense. "Keeping the Sabbath holy" is tough for me, because I work in a church. You'd think it'd be a piece of cake—I'm in a house of worship every week at this time, so what's the problem?

I am the problem, or rather, my scattered brain is.

The Sunday School/Confirmation Class hour is busy in the extreme. I try to arrive at church at least an hour early to prepare for the onslaught of little darlings at 9:00, and I still feel unready, often. The 90 minutes before service often feel like lots of God-talk without a heckuva lot of God-contemplation.

As I dart into church after leading the Sunday School gathering, my pious thoughts run to my mic for the children's message (will it work?) and the $30 cash pressed into my hand as I pass a pew (for bingo? the youth group outing? our Sunday School charity project? Who just gave that money to me, anyway?) When Ken begins the organ prelude, I am still having whispered conversations about the bake sale after service. During the announcements, I'm always kicking myself for items I forgot to ask Pastor Kay to mention. The opening hymn is a fine time to wonder if I turned off the projector down in Confirmation class. And nothing like hearing the

Gospel to remind me that I forgot to order new curriculum for next quarter. At Communion, I reverently ponder whether I replaced the acolytes I'm taking to the mosque next week.

Many Sundays, I drive home and realize I've done everything at church BUT worship God.

This past weekend was a shining example of my "faithlessness." I was asked to be chaplain for the synod junior high youth gathering out near Lancaster. This three day extravanganza involved two sets of retreaters (Friday/Saturday and Saturday/Sunday groups), a total of 220 6th-8th graders. My duties included, but were not limited to, designing and manning a prayer center for the kids, as well as leading worship and preaching at two services. Aside from the fact that I felt like a bit of a fraud, being neither a pastor nor a seminary graduate (the planning team was desperate), I also spent the weekend in a constant state of anxiety. Would the film clip leading into the sermon play correctly? Did I bake enough communion bread to go around? Would the young participants "get" the ideas behind the prayer stations or would they just be a chance to play with clay and punch holes in paper dolls? By the time we waved farewell to the last carload of tweens and finished cleaning up the camp, I felt like I'd run a marathon. It was only much later that I even thought to thank God for His invaluable help and guidance.

I'm sure others have similar distractions at times, but for me this is a constant problem. And it's further evidence that, so much of the time, I'm only half there, wherever I am. The rest of me is a) off in a mental corner, berating myself for my myriad missteps and mistakes b) making shopping lists c) generally woolgathering: hmmm, if I paint the kitchen cabinets white, I need to repaint the kitchen walls a different color—or do I?

Lord knows I try to focus (I really believe He does know), but it feels like a losing battle, especially on the one day we are asked to step off the treadmill of the work week. All too soon, it's Sunday night again—I'm ready to launch into another Monday, having taken not a minute to meditate or calm myself or even really think about my loving Creator.

I've (very) recently started taking Thursdays off. My goal on these days is to do no "church" work, but to read, write, have lunch with friends, etc. I sleep a little longer, and linger over my coffee. I'm thoroughly enjoying this total change of pace. And I'm wondering: can Thursday be my new Sunday? Can I stop beating myself up because it's hard to focus on the "Sabbath," and instead carve out my unique moments to rest and spend some time with God?

It's worth a try.

MASTER OF THE UNIVERSE

"I have only one superstition... touch all the bases when I hit a home run."

--George Herman (Babe) Ruth

OK, since it's just you and me here, I'll share a secret with you: I have ultimate power. I can make things happen. I can also keep things from happening. How do I do it? Simple: I wear my lucky earrings. I sleep on the left side of the bed. I eat the same yogurt breakfast every day. As long as I stick to these rituals, all will be well. Do you want your sports team to win? Do NOT allow me anywhere near the field of play. One glance from me is enough to send the opponent's score skyrocketing. Do you want your beautiful outdoor wedding to go off without a hitch? Remove me from your guest list or prepare for a deluge. On the other hand, make sure I'm concentrating on you, and am clad in my lucky sweater, if you want to ace your SATs. Bring me along, sitting of course in my lucky fifth row center seat, to ensure a brilliant concert performance.

I learned of my special powers in first grade. My first day of school, I accidentally boarded the wrong bus home. Dad had brought me on a regular New York City bus in the morning. In the afternoon, as I climbed onto the rather different big orange vehicle, I noticed that there were no advertisements for Seagram's Whiskey inside, nor was there a charge to ride. Hmmm. The principal, Sister Agnita, discovered my error, clambered aboard and yanked me out of my seat, chastising me all the way to the curb. On several other occasions that year, Sister A appeared the second I did something wrong—like committing the cardinal sin of going to the main office for the SSR (sustained silent reading) materials 10 minutes before I was supposed to run this errand. She literally screamed at me. I was terrified of her. When summer came at last, I began to pray, earnestly: "Please God don't let Sister Agnita come back in September!" I had spoken, and my wish was apparently the Almighty's command. In July, my Nana was reading the *New York Times* on the porch at the beach. "Elise, wasn't your principal named Sister Agnita? I'm reading her obituary!" Wow!! I had killed her with my thoughts!!

From then on, I was a force to be reckoned with. As I grew, I noticed my control over life's ups and downs increased. If I played the Beatles' "Rubber Soul" album while I was writing a paper, I was guaranteed an A. "Abbey Road" wouldn't do at all. It was uncanny—not only did what I wore, ate and listened to determine the future—saying certain things at certain times also seemed to make a difference. For example, I felt the motorists in my life were always protected, as long as I was there upon their departure to say these precise words: "Drive safely—don't let me worry about you!" When my Steve once left abruptly for work, I actually ran after his car, shouting my magical phrase. Better safe than sorry!

These days, I arrive at my church job at 8:15 AM (not 8:14, not 8:16) to ensure smooth sailing (after putting on those lucky earrings and drinking three cups of coffee—not two, not four). I end every phone call to my children with "I love you," even when it seems comically inappropriate to do so: "PJ, you left the kitchen a mess. You forgot to take out the trash. You didn't mail the package I needed you to mail. I love you, PJ."

There are times when I wonder if I really do wield all this influence over destiny. Is it a fact that I am singlehandedly responsible for the weather? Would the kids have been accepted to college if I had not been the first one at the mailbox to see the admissions letters? Does my choice of coffee cup truly change the course of my day?

Is it possible that I am just a superstitious nut?

Possible, perhaps. But why take a chance?

Sunday will be a big day at work. Better wear my lucky red high heels. Then I'll be all set.

GROWING, GROWING, GONE

"You can get what you want or you can just get old."

--Billy Joel

I had lunch with my friend Susan yesterday. We've known each other since the kids were babies. Susan remembered that our family had always hung our stockings on the mantel for St. Nicholas Day She asked if we were still doing that. We're not. With only Julie now here on Dec. 6th, it didn't seem to make sense to fuss over a Christmas stocking for one 17 year old. Last night, I didn't make my customary dash to the mall to load up on last-minute stuffers. This year, and probably from now on, today is just another ordinary day.

Every year, we bought an ornament for everyone to hang on the Christmas tree, then keep in boxes of their own until they moved away. Sheridan, Evan and Rosie are each unsettled on a permanent residence, so we still have theirs (though Steve and I have to hang them up). Yule-loving PJ grabbed his box last year and took it to college at Millersville, where he decorated a small tree in his dorm. It won't be long before our annual evergreen is completely bare (we couldn't afford to buy ornaments for ourselves).

Christmas morning was another ritual—opening the gifts slooowly, one at a time (which prolonged the magic, and made not-so-many presents look like the mother lode). Even so, cumulatively we could have opened a branch of Toys R Us, with our jillion Legos and Playmobils, our puppet stage and Brio train set and play kitchen. Recently, as Sheridan and his wife Ya-Jhu are both church music directors with major Christmas AM obligations, we've waited till nearly noon for the gift-opening ceremony; it's still fun, but has lost a bit of the luster of the old days (how rhapsodic can one wax over pounds of gourmet coffee and practical scarves?)

We still serve breakfast in bed to any birthday children still at home, but it's not the same as it used to be. When all five of them were small, we'd each contribute something to the breakfast tray—a pretty flower, a Beanie Baby, a crayoned card. Then we'd add the plate of French toast, and up the stairs we'd troop, singing "Happy Birthday" in what we thought might possibly be harmony. We have many photos of the young honored ones, sleep-tousled but thrilled, sitting up in bed eating their special meal. Things got tricky after they hit middle school and had to leave earlier in the morning. By the time high school (6:45 AM!) rolled around, we'd be scrambling the eggs madly, stuffing a flowering weed from the yard into a vase, and racing pell-mell through the birthday song as Anniversary Boy or Girl nervously watched the clock lest he/she miss the bus. Lost a little something over time.

My children are growing, growing, gone. And I put away their childish things, eyes tearing up. While the days seemed endless when they were still in diapers and wouldn't share their toys and NEVER napped...looking back, it was a ridiculously short span when I had them all home together. I did, on some level, know how lucky I was, but I'll always wish I had taken the time to savor the moments more. I took for granted that there would always be tiny guys around to make birthdays and Christmas times of such excitement, wonder and joy.

While I am waaaay too young to be a grandma (of course), I look forward to sharing magical childhood moments with precious little ones again someday.

Meanwhile, it's December 6th, and I'm feeling kind of blue. St. Nicholas skipped our house this morning, and I don't think he'll be back.

FELLOW TRAVELERS

Q: What is the difference between an introverted and an extroverted Lutheran?

A: An introverted Lutheran looks down at his shoes while he is talking to you. An extroverted Lutheran looks down at YOUR shoes.

I'm about to get all Garrison Keillor here: I get a charge out of Lutherans.

At church Maundy Thursday, Pastor Kay and I set up two washing stations—one for feet, one for hands. Hand washing had been introduced last year as an alternative practice for those too modest to display their tootsies, and it was a hit. This year my station (the feet) had exactly one customer, whereas the line for hands was quite long. Several times, folks who didn't want to wait came over to me and asked ME to wash their hands. Well, that does it. We've decided to bag foot washing altogether next year.

It's ironic, because this tradition is all about humility (Christ washing the disciples' feet) and if Lutherans are anything, it's humble. From their propensity for sitting in the back pews, to their reluctance to toot their own horns in general, you'll find most Lutherans fading into the woodwork when folks of other denominations take center stage. For many years, the evangelism committee at Christ's Lutheran had an annual budget of almost zilch, and rarely spent it. Why badger people to come visit our house of worship? If they really want to find us, they can look us up themselves! We won't turn them away!

In this respect, the Seyfrieds probably make lousy Lutherans. Almost all of us have gravitated towards "look at me" professions—acting, music, writing. PR is a specialty of our family. I like to think our egos are not too outsized, but we sure do have healthy self-images. My dear church family has embraced our "otherness" and seems relatively tolerant of our bunch (though I'm sure they shake their heads from time to time at our very public antics). We are the quintessential front pew sitters, and never turn down an opportunity to stand up and speak up, both in and out of church.

It took a little while for us to get acclimated here. At Christ's Lutheran, we sing most, if not all, verses of the hymns (for Catholics, two verses mean it is Christmas or Easter), and we stay until the very very end of the service (as a Catholic, an often heard post-communion motto was "receive and leave.") To me, the Lord's Prayer ended at "but deliver us from evil," fish was what you ate on Friday, and confession was something you did in a booth.

And now look at us.

Misfits though we may be, the Lutheran church really means a lot to our family. The belief in the sufficiency of God's grace, grace overflowing into every aspect of our lives, that we don't have to do a thing to "earn," has a powerful appeal to Steve and me. Lutheranism has been called Catholicism without the guilt. I will not take potshots at Catholics (after all, I was one for decades); I will merely say that I find the idea of Heaven as God's gift <u>already</u> given, quite wonderful.

Every believing family makes a choice—in which faith do we want to raise our children? I don't really think there are any wrong answers: God loves us all, whatever path we travel to Him. The important thing is to find a spiritual home where we can worship surrounded by the people we care about, and who care about us. We Seyfrieds cast our lot with our quiet, retiring, wonderful Lutheran friends, people who have received us with the kind of grace and open-heartedness with which God receives us all.

And who do coffee hours and soup suppers up right.

A MATTER OF TRUST

"The best way to find out if you can trust somebody is to trust them."

--Ernest Hemingway

For more years than I care to admit, I left my front door and my car unlocked all the time. In a neighborhood of beautiful homes, who would bother with This Old House? If someone did, I imagined the would-be robber surveying the contents (including an 18-year-old TV and an assortment of cheap costume jewelry) and leaving us a few items out of pity. And what self-respecting thief would lust after a bottom of the line Hyundai with scratches, dents and coffee-stained seats? I think of gasoline as "good to the last drop" and therefore the tank is usually almost empty, so the stolen car would sputter to a halt at the end of the driveway anyway. I was sure we were well under the radar screen when it came to breaking and entering.

There was, I believed, safety in dilapidation. I thought of myself as a trusting soul, who daily appealed to the outside world's better nature, and for the longest time my luck held out. In reality, I was more lazy than trusting, living in a la-la land where everyone kept their mitts to themselves.

But all that changed recently. In the span of four months, my wallet was stolen (from church!) and my Facebook account was hacked. My habit of leaving my purse within easy reach of anyone entering the building was my undoing in the first case. In the second, I'm guessing my habit of using the same "weak" password for my every online account (why bother to memorize a bunch of letters and numbers?) made

Mr. Hacker's job an easy one. In both cases, not much damage was done (I hope my wallet-snatcher enjoyed his $35 shopping spree), except the damage to my faith in mankind.

So now I am hyper-vigilant. I hide my purse in my office in places so obscure that even I can't find it. I now have an encyclopedia of computer passwords. House and vehicle are locked tighter than drums. And even with all these precautions, I don't feel safe anymore. Every stranger, from the six year old in the park to the gray-haired granny on the train, looks highly suspicious to me (oh yes, granny! I'm on to you and your clever disguise!) So I avoid making any contact with those I don't know. When I left my ancient cell phone at the library the other day, my immediate, but erroneous, thought was that it had been swiped (even though mine is such a stripped down model that you practically have to dial it). I cling to my "stuff" for dear life, and that life is now a buttoned-up, battened-down one.

I've been thinking of two women I love very much lately: my late sister Maureen and my younger daughter Julie. Though they never met, the two have a great deal in common—including vast amounts of trust. Both of them never met a stranger, and ended any trip to the store or on public transportation by making a new friend. Theirs is/was not foolish trust; the appropriate locks have always been secured. But both Mo and Jules have sought—and found—the best in people. They've never feared encountering others. As a result, 30 years after her death I still hear from folks I don't really know, who remember my sister with love. Julie has a huge array of buddies from all walks of life.

Is there danger in this open-hearted approach to being? Of course. But I now err on the side of caution to a ridiculous degree, and still feel threatened. The danger here is closing myself off, assuming the worst of my fellow man, losing the desire—and finally the ability—to relate to the stranger. My big wide world is rapidly shrinking, and I hate it. But I despair of turning back, of opening myself up again. Too risky. Better to clutch my belongings and stare straight ahead on the street. Better to assume just about everyone is up to no good.

And I have to be frank—there are MANY times I don't trust God any more than that shady-looking man on the subway. I don't trust that God is at work in my life, don't trust that He has things under control. I place all my trust in me to do the heavy lifting, and—surprise, surprise—I regularly let myself, and others, down. Most people are kind and honest, and when I stop trusting I stop seeing that; stop seeing God in the stranger's face.

I may have all my "riches" secure, but my life is much the poorer if I choose fear. So let me take a page from Mo and Julie's notebook. Let me make contact—eye contact, heart contact—with people again. I'll take the necessary precautions, but after that let me relax. Trusting in a beautiful world, one filled with friends I just haven't met yet.

TAKE A NUMBER

"We exist in chronos. We long for kairos. That's our duality. Chronos requires speed so that it won't be wasted. Kairos requires space so that it might be savored."

--Sarah Ban Breathnach

I rarely visit the deli counter at the grocery store, and I finally figured out why. I hate to take a number and wait. My husband and children are thus deprived of their pastrami and provolone because it might, oh horrors, take five minutes for me to be served. That is five minutes of my life that could be profitably spent doing something else (never mind that "something else" is frequently "staring off into space trying to remember where I left my glasses, and finding them on top of my head").

I totally dread doctor appointments for myself and the kids. Yes, I dread them because I read all the medical horror stories on the Internet, about ingrown toenails that lead to amputations, early signs of Alzheimer's (losing glasses), etc. etc. But the real reason I dread them? I have to wait. And wait. And wait. Because I always forget to bring a book (see early signs of Alzheimer's), I am left to enjoy *Highlights for Children*, or *People* magazine from June 17, 2003. One time at the pediatrician's, Evan and I were finally ushered in to the cubicle at the very back of the office, where we waited. And waited. And waited. And finally emerged to find that everyone had gone home and the cleaning crew was vacuuming.

I've always been impatient. When I was a child I was out-of-my-mind impatient to grow up. While my peers were happily amusing themselves with Chatty Cathy dolls and hopscotch, I was not-so-happily biding my time, eager for the day I could drive, and vote, and stop sitting at the kids table on Thanksgiving.

Pregnancy was a trial for me, not because I had any complications, but because I wished for the gestation period of a hamster. From the positive test on, I had my due date in laser focus and willed myself to get through the endless weeks ahead. I was appalled that one measly baby took so long to make an appearance! The fact that maternity wear in those days was all kinds of hideous didn't help. I still cringe at photos of me, a grownup, wearing huge tops with enough cutesy bows and ruffles to outfit an entire ballet class.

I'm not much better waiting for my prayers to be answered, to be honest. From the moment I mutter "Amen" I expect the heavens to part, harps to play and The Solution to appear before me. Sometimes I'll give God as long as a week (I'm a reasonable sort) before I start to grumble and grouse. Hello! I'm WAITING! Come on, Mr. Omnipotent, get busy! I feel like I'm taking a number (number 50 billion) at the Divine Deli Counter, and I just want to skip to the front of the line. After all, I'm praying for good things, for myself and others— a return to health, a new job, a safe trip. So what's the hold up?

But recently I've started thinking a bit differently, and it's all because of kairos time.

The Greeks have two words for the concept of "time": chronos and kairos. Chronos time is, no surprise, chronological time (it's 12:30, it's Wednesday). The definition of kairos time is more subtle. Kairos can be called the "perfect moment" for something to happen—the moment, whenever it is, in which God acts. In chronos time, I fuss and fume when the repairman is late, when the Confirmation class straggles in well after 9 AM. I'm trying more these days to be conscious of kairos time. Kairos time exists beyond clocks and stopwatches and my drumming fingers. I trust that God hears me exactly where I am, and values my prayers. But I also believe that God operates in kairos time, and answers my prayers at just the right moment—impossible as that may be for impatient me to understand. How many times over the years have I looked back later and been grateful that I did NOT get what I prayed for? Many. And even when the "no" answer continues to be painful, I'm learning (slowly) to trust that all will be well in God's time, if not in mine.

I believe that the dead are not far away at all, that they live on just out of our reach. I believe our departed loved ones watch over us and actively love us still. And I believe that their time is, always, kairos time.

What would my life look like if I stopped dwelling on the ticking of the clock? What if I started thinking of life and afterlife as a seamless whole, with kairos moments all over the place, when one form of our existence touches the other? What if I stopped imprisoning Reality within the narrow confines of my grasp of it?

Next trip to Shop'N Bag, I think I'll take a number, grateful to be where I am, slowing down to smell the chicken salad and pickles, lucky to be able to purchase food to feed my beloved family.

God grant me the serenity…to wait.

WHERE TO?

"A man's mind plans his way, but the Lord directs his steps."

--Proverbs 16:9

I've always had a lousy sense of direction. Even as a child, I remember getting lost on a three block walk to a friend's house. Whenever anyone asked me where my school was, for example, I drew a complete blank. Perhaps the other kids were paying heed as our intrepid driver careened through the neighborhoods in Bus 22 towards Our Lady of Perpetual Help. Not me—the bus could have sprung paddles and propelled us across the water to London every day for all I noticed or cared.

It didn't help that we moved around a lot. New York City and suburbs, Duxbury MA, Atlanta GA...it was all a blur of expressways, residential streets and winding country roads. Dad was the family chauffeur, and I was constantly amazed when we pulled up to the library or grocery store. *How the heck did we end up here?* I'd think. Every single time.

When I reached age 16 and got my license, I thought I might magically master the twists and turns that would lead me to my destinations. Alas, no. The map (remember the roadmap?) was my constant companion whenever I strayed from my habitual route to work—and forget about detours! I should have traveled with a bag of breadcrumbs, à la Hansel and Gretel, to mark my path. Inevitably, I'd pull into a gas station, hopelessly turned around, listen intently to the cashier's instructions—then take off again in the opposite direction from what had been recommended seconds before.

Getting older, it's gotten worse. For some reason, even if I can get somewhere, I get all befuddled when it's time for the return trip. Nothing looks familiar, no landmark rings any kind of bell with me. I blame my chronic inattention to my surroundings. By the way, don't ask me the color of your carpet or the make of your vehicle—I haven't a clue.

My mom Joanie never drove, and gabbed her way through life in the passenger seat, Mrs. Oblivious. God help you if you asked her to find a location. She would look at you as if you'd just requested a short-cut to Jupiter. Luckily Mom never had to find her way out of a paper bag on her own.

Among my offspring, Rose, PJ and Julie can navigate pretty well on the highways and byways. They can find IKEA without ending up at Walmart. Sheridan is spooky: for a non-driver, he can lead anyone anywhere with 100% accuracy. But Evan is my Traveling Twin. He was born and raised in Oreland and still has trouble finding his way around. We thought it quite ironic that he was charged with driving a submarine in the Navy, and often pictured the boat heading the wrong way around the world with Ev at the helm.

Steve is Directions King, hands down. He can find a place he hasn't driven to in 30 years. He NEVER gets lost. I find him very obnoxious.

I watched a video the other night by the terrific young writer and pastor Rob Bell, called "Shells." In it, Bell talks about Jesus' perfect sense of direction and purpose for his life on earth. He was, always, traveling towards Jerusalem and the cross. That was his goal, his "one thing" to which all of his other activities (healing, preaching) led Him. Rob compares our journeys, with all of our cares and distractions, to a child at the beach, holding two brimming handfuls of shells so tightly that he can't pick up the beautiful starfish that is within his reach. Bell challenges us to identify our "one thing," the main focus of our lives—our starfish, as it were—and to follow a pathway that leads us there.

I worry that my automotive directionless-ness has a parallel to my off-road existence. Am I drifting through the years without a clear sense of where I'm bound? Do I have a five-year—heck, a five-day—plan for my future? Am I always asking for help, then roaring off the opposite way?

I fear I may get to the final moment of my earthly span and say, "How the heck did I end up here?"

Lord, is it too late to develop a sense of direction?

DON'T PLAY GAMES WITH ME!

"By playing games you can artificially speed up your learning curve to develop the right kind of thought processes."

--Nate Silver

Want to get rid of me, pronto? There's an easy way: just suggest playing a card game. If I hear the words "500 rummy" or "hearts" or, Heaven forbid, "pinochle," I will be heading for the hills in no time flat. When it comes to playing—not to mention winning—any contest involving a deck, I am the human Two of Clubs (that's the lowest one, right?)

I simply cannot get card rules into my thick skull. As a child, I never even got the hang of Old Maid, or Go Fish, and I truly stunk at solitaire. Later on, when the gang gathered around for a hand or two of poker, I was clueless and, soon, chipless as well. It amazes me to hear my Steve explain complicated game instructions to the uninitiated. Every time he enlightens a would-be player, and I am within earshot, I listen yet AGAIN, swearing that this time I'll retain the value of the King of Diamonds, and remember what in the world a "trick" is. And every single time, the mere act of sitting down at the table facing my opponents wipes my brain clean. I struggle to get into the rhythm of picking up and discarding, and as for counting points—forget about it! Well, I take that back. It is always very easy to count my points. Think of the worst score you can imagine, and then go ten steps down. As a result, I soon lose interest. My mind wanders to tomorrow's dinner, or the new scarf I have my eye on. When my reverie is interrupted by "Elise? Elise? Your turn!" I take another embarrassing stab at making the correct move. Cards, for me, are a form of convivial torture—and who wants to be tortured, even convivially?

Sad to say, my gaming incompetence extends far beyond hearts and spades. I'm a sorry Sorry! player, go quickly bankrupt on Ventnor Ave., and have never even attempted chess. When the little ones arrived, I couldn't wait for Evan to be old enough to become a Candyland partner for Sheridan; playing board games with my children ranked right down there with diaper changing on my list of Dreaded Mom Chores.

Looking back, I can see exactly who on the family tree to thank for both my aptitude and attitude—my mother Joanie. Mom had ADHD ages before the term was coined, and the attention span of a gnat. She couldn't sit still for a TV show, she couldn't stay focused at Sunday Mass, and she was the worst game player ever (yes, worse than me). She made an attempt one time to join a bridge club, and spent the entire game gabbing away, as the über-serious aficionados frowned, then finally asked her to PLEASE be quiet and just PLAY. That, of course, was the end of bridge for my mother, forever.

Husband Steve's clan were all, by comparison, veritable card sharks, and loved to spend the lion's share of each family reunion dealing out Jacks and Queens and Aces to each other, keeping score laboriously, having a grand old time. Our kids inherited the Seyfried prowess; they have easily mastered an encyclopedia of games, and really enjoy playing them all. And although they graciously endure my infrequent attempts to join them, their sighs of relief when I drift away are rather audible. As I return to my book, I hear the intensity resume—shouts of victory, grumbles of defeat, and lots of strenuous card slapping on the table in between.

I've wondered, over the years, what the deal is with me and this type of competition. In other areas of my life I don't usually shy away from a challenge, but in this arena I do shy away, big time. I get nervous and flustered. I hate to lose, and I hate knowing that fact ahead of time. I was losing at Uncle Wiggly to Rose, consistently, when she was only five. The odds of my cleaning up at the blackjack table in Vegas are pretty poor.

I tell myself, "it's only a game," and "everyone has different talents," but still it bugs me that I can't learn to enjoy something that is such a great pastime for the rest of my family. I already opt out of 90% of their bowling, 99% of their hiking and 100% of their biking. Sometimes it feels like I'm missing a really big boat: the chance to do simple and fun things together, especially now that the kids are almost all grown and rarely around as a group.

It's my pride, I've concluded, that is holding me back, that keeps me from relaxing when I mess up. My husband and children are not a firing squad. On the contrary, they are my cheerleaders, always, in Battleship as in life. And if it doesn't matter that I lose miserably at cribbage, doesn't that free me up to laugh at myself? And if I'm free, maybe I can keep those nutty rules in my head—or enough of them to stay in the game.

So, OK, OK.

Deal me in, guys.

MY MOUTH DROPS CLOSED

"Nana will be so proud of me that her mouth will drop closed."

--Maureen Rose Seyfried, 1993

You're a character, Rosie.
But then you've always been one.
A flood of memories of small "Mo." You wanted to grow up to be "a clown, a farmer, or a recess aide." Your reaction to being sent to your room: "I'll go, but only if you'll let me SLAM MY DOOR." Your ability, even at age 6, to shock: "Mom, you know what I think is a great idea? Teenager pregnancy!" You went to what you called "reform school" (actually Reformed Church Nursery School. That one raised a few eyebrows). You were your parents' boon companion, even when you weren't quite sure what was going on: "Daddy and I are watching the golf on TV. Somebody just got putts. But I didn't see them. Actually, I don't know exactly what putts is." You were a preschool poet: "The rain carries the wind until it gets tired. Then it falls down." You had times of high and low self-esteem: "I'm confident because I'm competent." "I 'bust' myself first so no one else gets a chance to."
You were a tiny spitfire with eyeglasses and bangs. As my third child, but first girl, you had many of the traits of a firstborn: bossy, opinionated, critical, perfectionist. I can say that because I'm a firstborn too. Your relationships with your older sibs were sometimes fraught with conflict. You and Evan, in particular, interacted like an incredibly dysfunctional married couple; he would tease, you would fly off the handle;

you would pout, he would tease, and round the mulberry bush we went. While you were basically patient and loving with little PJ and Julie, you had no real interest in playing baby games.

Even though I wanted to throttle you at times, there was no denying your off-the-charts cuteness factor. I don't know if it was the specs (you needed them from age 2, after eye-muscle surgery), or your low throaty voice, so jarring coming from such a little peanut...whatever it was, you won my heart, big time, and nothing ever changed that.

Fast-forward through middle school (wish that had been an option!) You decided that you were a) a traveler and b) a businesswoman. You opened Bon Mo Desserts, and sold really delicious homemade cookies, cakes and pies to our hungry neighbors. These goodies funded trips to London and Jamaica (what 11 year old takes her mother on vacation to Jamaica? Mine!) and whetted your appetite for more far-flung adventures.

At a very tender age, you began singing. In church you were part of a small group of vocalists called Stepping Stones; in school you sang in chorus and, over the years, scored many solos. One summer you went to Westminster Choir College camp. Then you joined the Temple University Children's Choir, and adored the freedom of riding the train by yourself into center city for weekly rehearsals. With each new experience, your voice strengthened and grew more beautiful.

High school brought your year in Thailand (and your name change to Rose, your middle name); college brought an internship in London and time in Italy. During that period, you were a Starbucks barista, worked in the international admissions office at Berklee, and served as a Big Sister in Boston. We never lost touch, but it was clear you had to ration your precious and rare free time. As a mom, I understood. As your #1 fan, I wanted more.

And now I have it—in a way. Thanks to the magic of SoundCloud and YouTube, I can see/hear you often, performing original songs. Facebook keeps us in contact too, as I hear about your insane current number of jobs in NYC: audio engineer, Foley artist, composer, sound editor, singer and the list goes on. I just wish I could see you more often. Sometimes Brooklyn feels as far away as London. But I know you are happily busy building a career and a life. When you were a child, it often seemed like you were racing through your youth to become the adult you were born wanting to be. I'm so glad you've made it.

Through it all, you remain true to yourself. You are a strong, compassionate, capable young woman (and yes, still a little opinionated and bossy). Inside exciting New York Rose, there still dwells precocious Mo—the girl I fell in love with the day she was born.

I'm so proud of you, my mouth is dropping closed.

DIAL TONE

"All men's miseries derive from not being able to sit in a quiet room alone."

--Blaise Pascal

Me: "Hi, Evan!"
Evan: "Hey."
Silence
Me: "Evan, are you there?"
Silence
Evan: "Yeah."
Me: "I'm so glad to hear your voice!"
Silence
Me: "Evan, are you still there?"
Silence
Evan: "Yup."

And so forth. My telephone calls with my second-born son since he's left home have always had the pace and snap of a primitive communiqué from Alexander Graham Bell himself. In 10 minutes of painful repartee, I've usually been able to pry out the following information: he was alive, he was "good," things at school/work were "good" aaaannd that's about it.

I shouldn't have been surprised. Even as a toddler, Evan was a man of few words, usually letting big brother Sheridan finish his sentences (which the gabby Sher was ever-eager to do). On the phone he was hopeless. When he'd finished speaking with my mom long-distance from Atlanta (and the phone had been passed along to chatty little Rose), he'd run off to play like an inmate sprung from prison.

My favorite Evan telephone memory from school days was the time he had to call a girl (gasp!) to get a missed homework assignment. She was not there, so he had to (even worse!) leave a voicemail message. As he finished, he slammed the phone back on the receiver, buried his face in his hands and yelled, "Idiot! I sounded like an IDIOT!" Needless to say, he never missed a homework assignment again.

When Evan entered the Naval Academy, he had the perfect excuse not to call—during plebe summer, he basically wasn't allowed to. The freshmen were able to make only two calls, three minutes each. I imagine this suited my taciturn son down to the ground—by the time each member of our big family had said "hello" it was time to hang up.

When he was stationed in Hawaii, he was, shall we say, off the hook: none of us seemed to be able to keep track of the six hour time difference. When I was ready to talk, it was either 3 AM Honolulu time, or 2 PM, right in the middle of his workday. I assumed his infrequent calls were completely due to similar confusion on his part (right? Right?) When Evan's submarine was underway, of course, no calls were even possible. And even if he was a chatterbox, there was a lot he was not permitted to divulge—including all details of the boat's comings and goings (the when, the where—all off limits for discussion). No worries there; the Navy's secrets were utterly safe with our boy.

Now he is in Washington, DC, and while the physical distance has shrunk dramatically, the communication level has not measurably increased. I often rely on Facebook to keep track of even a few of his activities. Fourth of July fireworks on the National Mall? Dinner at a dear friend's house? Apparently, from photographic evidence, he was there. When I do catch him on the internet at the same time as I am, he is ALWAYS on his way out the door. Coincidence? I think not! I flash back to little Evan and those brief long-distance "hellos" with Nana. 20 years later, Ev's behavior is still utterly consistent.

One of the amazing things about parenting, especially rearing multiple children, is learning how different the kids all are, from one another and from me. While, alas, I do notice some of my un-lovelier qualities surface from time to time, they remain staunchly their own people, owning their traits and quirks. I am relieved, intrigued, and baffled, in equal measure. Where did their musical talent come from? How about Rosie's guts, forging her own path in the NYC world of sound design? Sheridan's patience, PJ's sunny nature, Julie's thoughtfulness and yes, Evan's circumspection? All gifts from God, not their mother.

I must say that in person, Evan has vastly improved as a talker, particularly when the topics are music (especially new bands) and, of all things, cooking. He's a wonderful cook now, and we can actually converse for a long time about kitchen tips and tricks. And he's always been a GREAT listener, which is quite a rarity in our yakkity-yakking house. He absorbs and remembers what we say, and his responses are insightful and to the point.

So what if he never changes? Does it matter that he dreads the ringing of his cell phone and emails only under duress? I'm guessing that Evan will remain quiet, inscrutable Evan, and that's OK with me.

But anytime he <u>does</u> reach out, I'll always be all ears.

...BUT FOR THE GRACE OF GOD

"To be a Christian means to forgive the inexcusable because God has forgiven the inexcusable in you."

--C.S. Lewis

My Rosie went to college in Boston, and often ran through its streets. She has scads of friends up there. My dear young friend Carrie is in school there now, and was actually at the Marathon. My first thought that terrible Monday was, "Is everybody OK?" Thankfully, everyone we know seems to be fine, physically if not emotionally. But a gaping wound was opened with those two explosions, and it will take a lot of time for that city to really heal. Who will be held accountable for this tragedy? A 19 year old boy. And in the end, what difference will it make? The lost cannot be returned. There are no do-overs when evil strikes. Nothing can be undone.

Last week at Sunday School gathering, I talked with the kids about forgiveness: Christ's mandate for us to pardon one another "seventy times seven" times, no matter what. Today, we had the opportunity to put our words into action. I gave the children pens and paper, and asked them to write two notes. One will go to Jeff Bauman, a double-amputee and the hero who helped identify the suspects for the police. Predictably, the children wrote letters of praise and encouragement to Jeff, and I know he will be cheered by reading them. The other? The other will be sent to the hospital where a young man named Dzhokhar Tsarnaev, fights for his life. He is responsible for three deaths and scores of serious injuries, all possibly in the name of some hideously twisted view of the

Muslim religion. His brother, by many accounts his mentor and the mastermind behind this heinous crime, is dead. So what do you write to a murderer?

Here's what they wrote: *Jesus still loves you. You did a horrible thing, but God forgives you. Change your ways. Get well. I'm praying for you.* Who knows if Dzhokhar will ever see these notes, and, if so, what effect they could possibly have.

Maybe, just maybe, these notes and others like them (my Lutheran colleague Rich Melheim came up with the idea and I hope many other churches will follow suit) will create a chink in his armored heart. Perhaps the seeds of reconciliation will be sown, and he will become, as Rich puts it, "the most loving person in prison." But even if he doesn't...

I hope the kids came to understand, even a little bit, that "there but for the grace of God go I"—go us. Any of us could have a child who turns to violence, a brother, a friend. Tsarnaev could BE us, given different circumstances—let's not kid ourselves about that. We are a hair's breadth away from the living nightmare we can cause for each other, we dreadfully flawed human beings.

Tomorrow I will mail both sets of letters, with prayers for both young men—the injurer and the injured. And I will continue to believe that no one, no one, is beyond redemption. With the grace of our endlessly loving God.

B – E – DOUBLE R – I – G – A – N SPELLS BERRIGAN

"Proud of all the Irish blood that's in me/Divil a man who'll say a word agin me."

--from "Harrigan" by George M. Cohan

I had (as all of us have) two grandpas. One, Pop Cunningham (Dad's dad) was something of a wastrel: 8th grade dropout, hard-smoking, hard-drinking, hard-living in general. Colorful as a set of 96 Crayolas, Pop was, to me, quite a character— fascinating but pretty unlovable.

Enter Pop's polar opposite: Mom's dad, Jack Berrigan. Fiercely loyal, friend to all he met. The original self-made man. Jack worked his way through college playing minor league baseball for the Bronx Giants. He had many a tale to tell. He once lost 20 lbs. during an August double-header in St. Louis; by the end of his baseball career he had broken every finger, at least twice. I have a photo of him with Babe Ruth. When he courted my Grandma, Rose Smith, she swore she would never marry a ballplayer (income too uncertain!) So Jack went to Fordham Law School, and shortly after graduation partnered with his brother Jimmy in a wild new profession: insurance. For some reason, this plan got the Rose Smith seal of approval, and they wed. Berrigan and Berrigan Insurance grew to be a most successful NY firm with many prominent clients.

I was only nine when Grandpa Berrigan died, but I have strong memories of him—cutting roses from his garden for us to take back to Manhattan after a Sunday visit to Larchmont, devising clever ways to baffle the squirrels (the bane of his existence), cheering baseball games on a black-and-white TV, mocking that new-fangled sensation, The Beatles (I wish I had a tape of his version of "I Wanna Hold Your Hand," which he titled "I Wanna Wring Your Neck").

Grandpa battled asthma all his life, back in a time without inhalers and other sources of relief. He would literally pass out trying to breathe. Indeed, when he died, it was because his heart exploded from his herculean efforts to get oxygen. At his wake and funeral, people from all walks of life, from bigwig executive to the elevator operator, talked about his kindness, his keen interest in their lives.

So I was proud of my Grandpa. But what sealed the deal were the vivid reminiscences of his offspring, my mom and uncles. His children remembered EVERYTHING about this man. The picture they painted was not of a saint. He struggled to relate to his youngest son Don, born with Down syndrome. He was rather strict, and young Jack and Gerry's Saturday morning chores would last all day long (clever man). He was often impatient with my rather wifty mom, his only daughter. Joanie was given to playing lots and lots of tennis at the country club. One time, Mom got sunburnt on the courts, and called for a ride home. "Did you ride your bike there? Well, that's how you can get home," replied Grandpa matter-of-factly.

But no one loved his family more, or worked harder to provide for them. He had come from a house full of brothers and sisters, with no money, and he swore he'd live differently. And he did. In later years, my mom, Uncle Jack and Uncle Gerry, past the age Grandpa was when he died, always waxed eloquent about Jack: "a piece of work," but one they adored.

Recently, Steve and I traveled up to Rye, NY to say goodbye to Uncle Gerry. He had lost a valiant fight against pancreatic cancer. My admiration for my uncle knows no bounds, and it was a privilege to be there with his children, three of my cousins: Meg, Gerry and Michele. When we left the cemetery, we all went to Westchester Country Club for lunch. We were joined by my Uncle Jack, the sole surviving member of that generation of Berrigans. I can't imagine how

Jack felt. Jack and Gerry were as close as my Sheridan and Evan, and it tears at my heart to think of any of them without their "other."

My cousins and I see each other, alas, mostly at weddings and funerals, and despite our vows to get our kids together it never seems to happen. This time, we swore on parting, would be different. We would see each other again soon, under much happier circumstances. And maybe it will happen. Who knows?

What I do know is that we are all aging, faster than we'd like. We are now the older Berrigans, the memory keepers. Those of us who don't resort to the dye bottle (I do) have gray streaks; we all sport a wrinkle or two. As the years gallop by (Mom used to say that, for older people, the weeks become weekends), we need to lasso the moments and savor them. Savor the laughter, and tears, of a shared past. We cousins are children of parents who had the same mom and dad. We are lucky to have each other, we Berrigans.

May I never take my family for granted.

FOR ALL THE SAINTS

"For all the saints who from their labors rest, Who Thee by faith before the world confess, Thy name, O Jesus, be forever blest, Alleluia! Alleluia!"

--William How

When I was a little Catholic girl, one of my favorite books was called *When Saints Were Young*. I got it as a First Communion present from my Aunt Rosemary. Anyway, it told the stories of the childhoods of famous and not so famous saints (St. Patrick, St. Thomas of Canterbury, St. Angela Merici). My favorite saint story from the book was that of St. Germaine of Toulouse, France. As a child she was mistreated by her stepmother and made to work outdoors as a shepherdess. Though dirt-poor, she was very devout, attending daily Mass (leaving her flock in a wolf-infested area—and they were never harmed), and praying on a rosary she had made out of string. How I longed to be holy like Germaine!! Minus the poverty and sheep-herding parts of course!!

In third grade I decided that sainthood was within my grasp, and thus began a rigorous program to become one of the blessed ones. Every night I played a record of Gregorian chants as I prayed and prayed, and waited for a vision (those saints all seemed to have visions). For good measure, I also hoped for the stigmata (wounds resembling those of Christ on the cross—St. Francis of Assisi was the first to have reportedly received the stigmata). That would be living proof that I was pretty darned special! Mind you, I still disobeyed my parents constantly and fought with my sisters to beat the band. But saints were once sinners too, I reminded myself. As long as I prayed myself into a trance nightly, aided by that other-worldly music, all would be forgiven.

Alas, my campaign for sanctity failed miserably. No visions, no flesh wounds, and the Gregorian chant record started to skip. I seemed incapable of curing anybody of disfiguring sores or even the common cold. It was with regret that I abandoned my quest and moved on to being an aspiring jet-setting ace reporter with a Barbie-style dream car.

When I became a Lutheran in my early thirties, I left the Catholic church, with a tinge of sadness that there was a plethora of saints I felt I could no longer pray to. We Lutherans tend to believe that we can eliminate the middle man—or woman—and talk with the Big Boss directly. Oh, I still invoked St. Anthony to locate my lost items, or St. Jude (patron of hopeless cases) when I was feeling, well, hopeless. But no more St. Christopher (safe travels), or St. Blaise (throat diseases), or St. Dymphna (mental health—and I could've really used her help there). The church system of verifying x-number of miracles in order to canonize people seems both arbitrary and bureaucratic. Who's to say if the blind man would have regained his sight without praying to this or that particular person? Are you telling me that Mother Teresa actually has to wait to become a saint?

Last Sunday was All Saints Sunday in church. As names were read of people who died in the past year, a bell tolled. We recognized that, flawed and falling-short as they may have been, they stand as saints in God's presence now. No need for a team of Vatican lawyers to validate. No toting up of beatific visions and wondrous acts necessary. Our dear ones, just by virtue of being loved by our God, are saints. Because, in the end, it isn't about what we do, because the best of us could never do enough. It's about what God does through us, each one of us, poor shepherdess and struggling spiritual formation director alike. Through God's grace our lives can become holy things, and by loving God we can become holy too.

May this Christmas bring you peace of mind and heart, as you reflect on the greatest miracle of all: God breaking into the world through His Son, for love of you. You, a sinner and a saint.

I'M GONNA MAKE YOU LOVE ME

"I'm gonna make you love me, oh, yes I will, yes I will."

--The Temptations

I was on the phone with my sister Carolyn in Hawaii recently. C confessed to being very bothered by something. Someone she'd thought of as a friend had suddenly turned ice cold and "dropped" her. I thought my sis was better off without this person, and told her so. But I completely understood her upset. It's how I live my life.

You see, I am a compulsive people pleaser. I come by it naturally. My mom Joanie couldn't bear to have anyone on earth dislike her. To that end, she was constantly bending over backwards to be warm and friendly and always agreeable. Mom, 70 years later, remembered, and OFTEN talked about, her failure to keep a classmate's friendship in elementary school. Apparently this child was a big stinker, but that didn't matter—little Joanie took everything she said and did incredibly to heart. Back when we lived in Massachusetts, our neighbor across the street took pleasure in switching moods on Mom: one day she'd be a delightful buddy, the next, a nasty adversary. Mom always blamed herself, and redoubled her efforts to please this un-pleaseable woman.

So that was my role model growing up, and I was an excellent study. As a result, my "friends" included a parade of girls who would invite me over to play, and then send me home in tears. I kept coming back for more, though, because my ever-shaky self-esteem ruled the day. In high school, I utterly exhausted myself in my quest to be universally loved.

It never once occurred to me that there might be people who wouldn't like me, even if I stood on my head and spit nickels. No, no—surely there was something I could say or do to win over the whole world!

Well, I haven't improved all that much. At 56 I still often yearn for complete acceptance by every soul I encounter. It's not just a matter of being generally nice to folks—there's nothing wrong with that. But when I obsess about people who, for whatever reason, don't care for me—well, that is a huge waste of time. And besides, do I think I'm so swell that the entire population has to find me irresistible?

My eagerness to please extends to my relationship with God, too. I know deep down that God's love for me is never-ending. And yet I still often think that I might disappoint Him so much that He'd finally give up on me, if not now, then after I die. The Catholic schoolgirl image of the Big Book of Judgment looms large, and I spend my life practicing delivering my own defense before the Almighty Throne. I envision I'd say what I often joke that I'd like written on my tombstone: "She Meant Well." Much as I love the concept of salvation by God's grace, clearly I don't buy into it 100%. I keep thinking that if I just throw in enough good works it will up my chances for a spot in Heaven. I don't quite trust enough, that I could ever BE enough.

And so on I struggle, plotting and planning to win the Heart that I won over before I was born.

But I am working on my issue, and there are small signs of progress. Oh, it still bugs me when I'm left off a guest list or snubbed in the supermarket, but I'm coming to learn that it's not all up to me. If other people have a Big Book of Judgment (and many do), and I fall short, so be it. I need to worry much less about my earthly popularity. And I need to worry much less about currying favor with God, because it isn't necessary.

Among my kids, I have a couple of people pleasers, and I hate that I've been a poor role model for them in this area. If I could give them one message today (and I need to remember this also), this would be it: just be yourself. God made us all unique, and loves us all, utterly and completely. So rejoice in your uniqueness. Revel in the people, and the God, who truly love you. For the rest, be nice, and if they still don't like you, let it go.

QUITTING TIME

"For everything there is a season, and a time for every matter under heaven."

--Ecclesiastes 3:1

My kids recently expressed sorrow that I finally stopped performing in our children's theatre productions. For some reason (wonder why?) they'd always enjoyed seeing their mother make a fool of herself onstage, fussing and fuming as the Wicked Queen in *Snow White*, "flying" and sword fighting as Peter Pan. I enjoyed it too, but now I've had enough. I've been playing these parts since 1979, when I was a mere slip of a girl, and it wasn't quite such a stretch to imagine me skipping down the Yellow Brick Road.

Before I met my husband Steve, I never really considered being an actress (though apparently I was such an overly dramatic child that I was dubbed "Sarah Heartburn"). I performed in the school plays, several of which I wrote. It was the writing, much more than the acting, that captivated me. But as Steve was a dedicated performer, and I was dedicated to Steve, I gravitated towards the theatre so that we could act together.

When Steve and I were young marrieds, it was just the two of us, hitting the road, and the stage, in hundreds of schools, libraries, recreation centers and theatres all over the Northeast every year. Looking back, I truly don't know how we did it. We averaged two or three performances a day, nearly every day, with travel in between. The show went on, through fevers and broken wrists and laryngitis. Along the way, we acquired endurance (our record: five shows in a single day). We developed thick skins, when the kids were either rowdy or—worse—eerily silent throughout the show. This often happened in Catholic schools, after Sister Mary Authoritarian, in her pre-curtain speech, warned everyone to be QUIET. Nothing quite as embarrassing as doing comic pratfalls and making jokes to pin-drop silence. We became flexible, as our venues ranged from huge auditoriums to a tiny space between library bookshelves. We learned to live and work together, 24/7, with a remarkable level of civility, even when my lousy map-reading took us three towns in the wrong direction when we were already late for a gig.

Eventually we settled down in Oreland, PA, but continued to keep up our hectic performance schedule. When it was time to begin our family, I breathed a sigh of relief. Surely I could take a much-needed break! But no! What's a little pregnancy anyway? No big deal! So it was back to work for Mom, well into the second trimester. I became an expert at concealment, donning ever larger and looser dresses so that the viewers weren't traumatized by the sight of Dorothy, six months along, waddling to Oz. And I'd be back at it two weeks after giving birth (still wearing the larger, looser dresses). We'd often bring a babysitter along to the show so I could feed my infant backstage mere minutes before going on. No wonder none of the five kids has chosen acting as a profession...they'd all paid their theatrical dues by the time they were toddlers!

For years now, I have been gradually bowing out of the shows, citing the demands of my other job at church and my ever-advancing age. We've hired many terrific (and a few not-so-terrific) young actors, who have been handling the bulk of the performances. Yet I have remained the go-to actress when Steve was in a pinch, largely because of my scary-good memory (in the script area only—in all other areas, the memory is scary-bad). With no rehearsal I could (literally) leap into *Toad's Escape* and sweep into *Cinderella*, without missing a beat. Little wonder, I guess, that my husband still depended on me to save the theatrical day. So, through my forties and early fifties, on I trooped when needed. Our young audiences, bless them, never commented on the fact that, clearly, Alice in Wonderland was as old as their grandmas.

But now I am, at last, truly finished with performing. I have hung up my crazy costumes for good, and retired my ruby slippers. I have kissed a large and very important part of my life goodbye. It was a heckuva lot of fun (mostly) while it lasted; now it's quitting time.

Learning when to stop is one of life's most valuable lessons. I pray, as I grow older, I can recognize all the other quitting times in my future. And make my peace with them.

STUCK ON YOU

"Though surely to avoid attachments for fear of loss is to avoid life."

--Lionel Shriver, *We Need to Talk About Kevin*

We are awaiting the arrival of Sheridan's buddy's cat. This mystery feline will be with us (Sher promises) only about two weeks, while its owner resettles. I am quite anxious about this, anxious about the climbing and the feeding and the (possible) clawing. But I'm also anxious that I might fall in a strange kind of love.

When Julie had her rabbits, I bemoaned their mess and smell. But the minute she returned them to the bunny rescue shelter, I keenly felt their loss. Ditto when hamsters Puffles and Truffles bit the proverbial dust: I actually shed tears at their passing. Bette the beta fish survives, long past her projected time of demise, and while she gives us zero affection, I know I will be sad when she goes to the big aquarium in the sky. I've always held the line at "NO dog," purportedly because I detest the idea of walking said beast in foul weather, etc. But honestly? I don't think I could stand to have a dog predecease me.

I get abnormally attached to the human visitors we seem to attract as well. When the kids bring friends home, for the holidays or just because, I take to them like a mother, and ALWAYS hate to see them go. Our foreign exchange students' returns home after short or lengthy stays were incredible wrenches (by the end of day two chez moi, face it, you are an honorary Seyfried). I pretend that I am thrilled for my youngest daughter, on the brink of travel and college and her exit from the house, but inside I just hate the thought of her leaving, just as I've hated the exodus of the older kids in their turn. I guess my ideal life would include a dwelling big enough for at least 20 or 30 people at all times.

Perhaps my holding on to the various creatures in my life is my way of freezing time. If nothing changes, I don't grow older. If something or someone leaves me or dies, I can't escape the fact that my days are numbered.

But so what if they are numbered? Why is that such a tragedy?

If I believe (and I do), that we are created for eternity, then what's the big worry? Why can't I consistently wrap my brain around the assurance that we will all be reunited in the end?

Because I want eternity right now (without actually dying, of course). I want to have lunch with my sister Mo, and ask my Nana to scratch my back again, and sit down for a long talk with my ever-chatty Mom. I want everyone I've ever loved within arm's reach, and I want them to stay there.

I know that's not possible yet, know that I have to wait until an unknown day in the future for the big reunion with those I've lost. And even after I die, I imagine I'll still be yearning for my children and grandchildren (and great-grandchildren) who remain on earth. I wonder: will it really be Heaven if the whole gang's not together?

Meanwhile, I wait for a cat, as I wait for all the new creatures, human and otherwise, who will be crossing my path in the days and years to come. I wait, with apprehension about their impending appearances, and expected sorrow about their inevitable departures. I wait for a cat, and every instinct tells me to harden my heart so I won't get hurt. Maybe the Buddhists have it right: a key to happiness is non-attachment.

But, try as I might to detach, that's not me. So I will no doubt continue to be an annoying clinger, completely wrapped up in all who populate my life. I'm probably doomed to stick to everyone like glue.

"Spring and Fall, To a Young Child" by poet Gerard Manley Hopkins, describes the grieving of a young girl, Margaret, at the arrival of autumn, and the falling leaves.

Hopkins ends with: "It is the blight Man was born for/it is Margaret you mourn for."

As I write this, spring is in the air at last. A cold and dreary winter, with unexpectedly late snowfalls, seems to be over. There is a bird perched in the tree right outside our family room window, and I can hear its rustling. The lawn is dotted with crocus and daffodil surprises (we haven't planted anything for years, and so are amazed when flowers come up anyway). And on this beautiful sunny day, I realize that I have a choice. I can love my loved ones, love my springs, while I have them, and not dwell on the inevitable autumns and winters ahead. I can love, with all my heart, and then let go when the moment comes. After all, it's Elise I've been mourning for—and maybe it's time to stop.

THE KEY

"Religion is like a map. The route isn't important. It's the destination that matters."

--Marianne Williamson

Where are they? Where are they? My typical morning routine features a frantic search of the house for my keys. Once located, they still migrate throughout the day from raincoat pocket to kitchen counter to front hall basket. I am convinced they spend their time clinking together, conspiring to drive me mad. Steve's keys are similarly subversive, so our typical leave-taking involves digging under sofa cushions, looking on top of the piano, checking every windowsill.

But my key adventures do not end there. I live in fear of locking myself out of my house. I also live in fear of locking myself out of my car, which in fact I did when Sheridan was a baby. Not only were the keys in the ignition, but the car was running. Thankfully, I'd gotten the baby out of his car seat before the fateful door slam. Still, it took time and a deftly wielded (not by me!) coat hanger to remedy things. I've also locked my keys in my office at church. I've lost the keys to the condo where we stay during the summer. I think what I need is a set of keys that look like the Fisher-Price colorful giant plastic ones that I can just wear on a chain around my neck. Even then, I'm sure I would find a way to misplace them.

Evan and PJ continue the family tradition, managing to lose keys with a frequency rivaling their mother's. There is a locked drawer in a desk that the boys had in their rooms. That there are valuable items in there, there is no doubt, but what? Pokemon cards? Probably. A real "pirate"coin? Possibly. An ossified pack of gum? Alas, we may never know, unless the key to the drawer magically turns up someday.

Even Rosie, the very soul of organization, managed to lock her keys in her Seattle apartment over Labor Day weekend. Thanks to good friends and good hearted neighbors, she was able to eat, sleep, and have clean clothes until her landlord returned from the holiday.

Locking things in implies keeping people out. Your treasures—your family, your home, your belongings— must be kept safe from intruders, from those who would steal what you love most. Yet you also dread being locked out, kept from your children, your cottage, your collection of Hummel figurines.

In Scripture, Eden was a totally open place, a Paradise where everything was in perfect harmony. Knowing humanity, I'm not surprised it didn't last long. Seems we've always broken others' trust, and distrusted each other. From time immemorial, we've coveted, then grabbed, what doesn't belong to us—and suspected others will do likewise. And so, we turn a key in a lock, and pray it will keep us safe. But then we lose our keys, and risk being painfully separated from the things we value. If we don't find them, we make new keys, and the cycle continues.

On a map, the key is a feature that orients us, helps us understand where we are and where we're going. Mountain, river, back road, interstate expressway—all have their symbols. It is within our power to study the key and find our way out of the wilderness. This key is not a locked door, but rather an open road. This key doesn't pen us in…we are free to explore the outposts, the remote trails, even the dead ends. This key entices us to live fully, charting our course and then setting out with confidence. We keep the map with us, folded in our pockets, as a reminder that we travel with help always nearby.

So what kind of key is faith?

Many would say that their faith is a special, safe, closely guarded place. A place that keeps out unbelievers, and any who would threaten it. For them, the key of faith is desperately clutched and, when misplaced, frantically sought until it is found again. But in life, keys often go missing. They remain on the hall table as their owners bang on the front door to get back in. They are bright little pieces of metal that stand between us and our world. And so faith can be a barrier to understanding. To daring. To trusting.

But what if we set our jangling keys down a minute, and picked up a map? What if we unlocked our hearts and opened them to a world of possibility? What if we saw life as a wonderful, terrible, amazing open road, and our faith as a tool to interpret it, a guide to appreciating it? If we stopped quaking in fear behind a locked door, what beauty could be revealed to us? If we have no set of keys to lose, perhaps we have everything to gain.

As I rush around each morning trying to locate the means to lock away my treasures, may I remember this: my Treasure is, always, unlocked, open to me—to all of us—every moment we draw breath. My Treasure doesn't languish on a chain, or hang on a hook, but leads me forward, into a world of risk and reward. My God is my map's key. May I learn to read Him, and learn from Him, and take comfort that He will never lead me astray.

May my faith, truly, set me free.

THIS OLD HOUSE

"The most expensive hobby a rich man could have is a boat, and the second most expensive hobby he could have is a very old house."

--*Barbara Corcoran*

I have no business owning a house. Especially an old house. Everything about its upkeep irritates me, and I resent every penny spent on it (and that's been many a penny). Nothing interests me less than cleaning, unless perhaps it's gardening, so our property is pretty neglected both inside and out.

Sometimes I picture trying to sell it, and the look of utter horror on the realtor's face as she looks around. Yes, I'd admit, the mammoth 40 year old air conditioner is still in the family room. We only turn it on when the temperature tops 90 degrees, because when we do it shakes the whole place and makes so much noise we have to shout to be heard. Yes, we still have only one (scary-looking) electrical outlet in the dining room. No, we have never replaced our drafty windows. Yes, we have been planning to refinish the living room floor since 1993. And yes, we're still living with tiny closets better suited for Tom Thumb's wardrobe. I'm pretty sure the agent's verdict would be: our ideal buyer will arrive with a sledgehammer and start all over.

Part of the problem, granted, is our ridiculously tight budget, but that's not all of it. I just really don't enjoy home ownership. My early years were spent in a New York City apartment, and as I recall it was Heaven. There was nothing to maintain; one quick phone call would get anything broken repaired. Best of all, when it was time to move, we could just close up shop and walk away.

As I grew older, and Dad took different sales jobs, we began relocating frequently. Over the years, we lived in three houses (New York, Massachusetts and Georgia) and several apartments. My parents were truly dreadful homeowners, like me, but we never lived in one place long enough to do much damage. Our happiest times were spent in recently built apartment complexes, where you could even call someone to come change the light bulbs (Mom actually did that). Atlanta was especially great because EVERYTHING there was new—new expressways, new mega-malls, new office buildings.

Our early married years were spent in an old apartment building on Lincoln Drive in Northwest Philadelphia. We'd looked in vain for the type of brand-new dwelling we'd been accustomed to down South. OK, OK, the Lincoln Drive place had its charms, but it also had its clanking heater, ancient bathroom fixtures and a rickety elevator I was afraid to ride. In Philly, we found, almost everything was on the older side, from the Schuylkill Expressway to the Acme supermarket. Maddeningly, this didn't seem to bother the locals in the slightest.

We've lived in Oreland since 1989, and the house predates that by a good 50 years. If these walls could talk, what stories they could tell, right? Sorry, but I prefer my walls to keep their mouths shut. Others might romanticize our abode, and note the fine craftsmanship of the entranceway, the beauty of the old trees on our property. Not me! Given my druthers, I'll take the very latest model every time!

So here I am, saddled with a house of a certain age. A house that, slowly but surely, is falling down all around me. A house that, now that I think of it, is a mirror image of myself—getting old, poorly kept up. I put off all general maintenance on me for as long as possible, and I know it'll only get worse with the flipping of each calendar page. Soon it will be AARP and senior discount day at the grocery store, and I hate the thought.

When I'm in shiny new spaces of stainless steel and glass, I can forget for a while that I carry quite so much history inside of me. I feel like I can wipe the slate clean and start again. But in my heart, I know I can't, really—none of us can. We can own the latest gadgets and live in a 2015 dream house, but the years catch up with us anyway.

I'll probably keep yearning for a sleek high-rise (and, honestly, a sleek young Elise), but for now this old house is my home. It's time to start taking care of us both.

STRANGER THAN FICTION

"It's no wonder that truth is stranger than fiction. Fiction has to make sense."

--Mark Twain

I don't know why, but lately a number of folks have asked me why I don't write a novel, a short story or another work of fiction. Perhaps they have read my books or blog and realize that they themselves are potential fodder for my next essay. Maybe they'd be more comfortable appearing in print in disguise.

The fact is, I did try my hand at a novel six years ago, in the throes of my manic depression. I wrote it in less than two sleepless weeks as part of the National Novel Writing Month challenge. The result, entitled *Stoppage*, belonged more in *Psychology Today* than on the *New York Times* bestseller list. It was up! It was down! It was up and down! I swear you needed Dramamine to read it. I can't bring myself to pick up *Stoppage* these days; too many unhappy memories of that tormented time in my life come flooding back. After that strange experience I swore off penning fiction for a while, returning to my factual comfort zone with relief.

But I remain intrigued by the possibilities of make-believe. While I'm standing in line at the supermarket, I'm inventing back stories about my fellow standers. Mr. Tenderloin may be frantically wooing the girl who is ready to leave him. Mrs. Giant-size Pampers is wondering if she can afford to buy food after she's taken care of her baby's diaper needs. The teens with the cart full of Oreos and Tostitos have the marijuana munchies. The dapper elderly gentleman with the solitary chicken breast and single tomato will go home to an empty apartment, with only Turner Classic Movies for company. It seems I should be able to parlay this natural curiosity, and my love of writing, into a piece of literature, yes?

Nope. Part of my problem is my severe ADHD. I simply cannot keep track of a plot, and often lose interest before I have even named all my characters. I read about successful authors who create complex charts detailing everyone's comings and goings, mapping out towns that only exist in their minds. I envy those who can hone in on Conflict and Resolution, and tailor a manuscript that brings both to life. One of my friends in my writer's group worked on a novel set in 19th century Rockport, MA for years, and recently finished it. Casey has a distinctive Victorian-era "voice," and I truly enjoyed reading her book. I just don't think I could ever go down that road myself. And yet...

And yet. How much of our lives are our own fanciful creations? As we shave or brush our teeth in the morning, don't we gaze into that mirror and decide who we will be today? Don't we dress in our costumes and enter into our plot? Perhaps the "real" tales I pen are actually a recounting of my made-up days.

I don't know about you, but I often stand on the blurry line between fact and fiction, wondering if I can believe my own eyes and ears. Amazing things occur, things that would stretch credulity on the printed page. My daughter Rose's casual coffee-shop conversation with a stranger in New York City led to the realization that the other person's cousin lives on the same block as we do in Pennsylvania. 30 years after my sister Maureen's death, I received an email from someone who had dated Mo back in the 1970s. He'd found and read my book while waiting in his doctor's office in New Jersey, and tracked me down. Hard to believe, but it really happened.

Someday I may give that novel another shot. Who knows? Meanwhile, I'll keep writing my truthful essays about my actual life, knowing that there is a world of mystery and fantasy contained within. And the next time someone asks me if I write fiction, I'll nod and reply, "Maybe."

THE BEST BIRTHDAY EVER

"There are two great days in a person's life - the day we are born and the day we discover why."

--William Barclay

My birthday falls three days before Christmas. When I was little I REALLY hated that. I never once had a birthday party. Instead I'd get a Merry/Happy combo gift from the relatives. And the household mood was always pretty grim. My mom was the grumpiest Santa imaginable, buying presents at the last minute, wrapping them poorly and shoving them under our Charlie Brown tree. And then Christmas dinner would loom. Mom was a chain-smoker who hated to cook (and had no taste buds left anyway) so putting together a meal that didn't involve Swanson's TV dinners was an ordeal. Who had time or inclination to make me a birthday cake too? Not Mom!

But as I got older, I started to enjoy the timing of my birthday. The Christmas festivities—the cards, the cookies, the carolers—all added to the fun of advancing to the next age. When the kids were little, I loved getting presents that they'd bought at the elementary school holiday gift shop: one year I got an "I Love Mom" pen, which didn't run out of ink for 15 whole minutes, plus a "Mom's the Best" dinner bell (which would have been useful if I was calling everyone in from the fields for chow), plus a "World's #1 Mom" coffee mug (not advised for hot liquids, I learned later).

Then came those milestone birthdays (35! 40!) that I dreaded. Who, honestly, WANTS to turn 50? I hoped that maybe if we just didn't mention it, it wouldn't be true. I tell myself "it's only a number," in which case, I'll pick number 21, please (surprisingly, that doesn't work.)

Once my chickies started leaving the nest, I only wanted one thing for my birthday: everyone home together. No need for presents and cake—they would be my presents, and sweeter than any cake. However, my heart's desire was much easier wished for than done.

Gathering even a majority of my children in one spot involves ridiculous logistics. The last time all five of them had been home at the same time was Labor Day, 2009—and that was a happy surprise. Rose was stuck in Boston (or so I thought). I called her just to say we would miss her, and as we talked, in walked Rosie, cell phone in hand. She had gotten a lift down with Evan. As always when everyone is here, there were many stories, and many laughs to share. As always, the visit was over much too soon.

Since that wonderful afternoon, group appearances of any sort had been like math problems: Sheridan + PJ + Julie - Rose - Evan; Rose + Evan - PJ - Julie - Sheridan; etc. There were people missing from the equation every time. Though I loved seeing them in any combination, I still longed to have them all, all at once. When would that happen again?

Our Evan is a Naval officer, and his schedule has always been the wild card. Last year, he asked for Christmas leave from Pearl Harbor, and, wonder of wonders, got it.

It was finally settled. The whole brood would be in one place for my 55th birthday. Since my children are musicians, several of them professionals, they decided to put on a benefit concert at church.

At 4:30 PM on December 22, I got my birthday gift. The last to arrive, Rose, walked in the door, and I had my five children, home for the holidays. To make things even more special, Ya-Jhu (Sheridan's fiancée, now wife) was with us as well.

The gang put on a great concert that night, but it was hard for me to focus on the music. I just sat and delighted in the sight of the Seyfried family. Together at last.

Beginning on Christmas Day, they scattered, back to jobs and school and their busy lives. I know that holiday reunions will always be a challenge. I have learned to treasure them whenever they occur.

I never thought turning 55 would be a joy, but it was. If I live to be 100, December 22, 2011 will still rank as my best birthday ever.

PHOTO OP

"Several people feel I have photographed God. Maybe."

--Alfred Stieglitz

Put that camera down, please.

No, I mean it. Really.

OK, you can take my picture, if you HAVE to, but if you post it online you're in big trouble.

I have always been photographically challenged. From the time I was gifted with a Polaroid "Swinger" camera at age 10, my victims knew that their photos would come out all blurry, or that the tops of their heads would be cut off. The next step after watching the film magically develop was always unceremoniously tearing the offending pic into little pieces.

And over the years my skills have improved not a whit. Ask me to snap a picture of you at the beach or, Lord help us, at your college graduation, and you do so at your own risk. When I finally figure out how to operate your camera, be prepared to hit the "delete" button because you will NOT look good. I guarantee it. I inevitably catch my subjects with mouths hanging open, or blinking, or grimacing. With my digital wizardry, I can transform even a supermodel into a frump.

My current camera has suddenly decided not to save every second or third picture. It's probably time for the repair shop, and yet I'm in no big hurry. I am absolutely positive the disappearing snaps are duds...my Canon knows best!

It's even worse when the lens is focused on me. I have one stock expression (smiling) that is tolerable, and so I try to be grinning whenever the paparazzi draw near, even at funerals.

Otherwise, the results are most unfortunate: it looks as if I am having a Bad Hair, Face and Body Day.

My sister Carolyn thinks she is very unphotogenic. Therefore, our albums feature everyone BUT her. C is usually off in a corner with a bag over her head, lest a shot accidentally include her. Carolyn believes she peaked, looks-wise, at about age four. Photographic records of her after that are rare. I'm amazed she agreed to pose for her wedding picture (she looked lovely, by the way). It would've been more like her to pose my brother-in-law Rob alone, with his new bride as the Invisible Woman.

My mom Joanie used to be equally camera-shy. The sad result, now that Mom's gone, is that we have precious few tangible reminders of her. What I wouldn't give to see more of her on film, even sporting that hideous hairpiece (a "fall") with the blond streaks. It's Mom! I wouldn't care!

On our family room walls hang very old photos, some dating back to the early 1900s. It was such a different time. Picture-taking was a rare event. Decked out in their finest, looking stiff and uncomfortable, Steve's grandparents sit, solemn-faced children on their knees, for a family portrait. My dad, at about nine months old, peeks out of an ornate baby carriage. I'm so glad to have these relics of the past, and when I look at them I like to imagine myself into their lives.

My kids are coming of age at the most visually documented time in history. The digital revolution has made photography ridiculously easy. It's not uncommon for one concert outing to spawn 100 or more cell phone pics ("There's Emily and me in front of the Electric Factory. Now we're making goofy faces. Now we're making goofy faces and pointing at each other.") These images are then loaded onto computers, where they are added to the hundreds of albums already there.

There must be a happy medium, between no pictures and a multitude, a place where my looking silly is OK. A place where C and I can be comfortable, whatever our facial expressions, knowing that the only reactions to our photos that truly matter are those of the people who love us. Looked at through the lens of love, anyone can be beautiful. Try it yourself with even unfortunate shots of people special to you—they look fine, don't they?

So go ahead, take my picture. I guess I don't mind too much after all. Someday, my grandchildren may see it, and remember me. And come on, sister C, get in the picture with me. Let's make goofy faces.

DO I HEAR A WALTZ?

"I won't take no for an answer/God began to say to me/when He opened His arms each night/wanting us to dance."

--St. Catherine of Siena

You would never think it to look at me on the dance floor, but I actually took lessons for several years—ballet and tap. These were to prepare me for my big theatrical break, when I would wow the director with my fancy footwork. There was just one little problem with my grand plan: I couldn't remember any steps. No matter how many times I repeated "shuffle hop step" in my head, or attempted a plié, my legs would have their own ideas. At auditions, it'd be even worse because I was so nervous. In the middle of a group of dancers, I was memorable only for being the one turning clockwise instead of counterclockwise. Needless to say, I didn't make the cut for *A Chorus Line*. The toe shoes and taps ended up in the trash, and I stopped trying out for musicals.

Socially, however, I've always loved to dance. In my early twenties I could even occasionally be seen in (gasp) discos. Again, I never mastered any particular steps, but in that setting it didn't really matter. It was just fun to move to the music. Over the years I stopped going out dancing, and it's a shame. Nowadays I trip the light fantastic only at wedding receptions, but I still really enjoy it.

A few minutes after Rose was born, she had her first dance. Steve held her in his arms and waltzed around the hospital room. It was a very sweet moment, as my husband got acquainted with his first daughter. We didn't take a picture, but the photo in my heart is still clear.

This winter in Taiwan, Julie, Ya-Jhu and Sheridan met Yaj's brand-new baby niece. This little one had been nicknamed "Lamby." At one point (and this was captured on film by Julie), Sher waltzed with Lamby around the room. When I saw it, I flashed back to Steve's father-daughter dance in October of 1988. I also flashed forward, to some future day when my son might be waltzing with his own daughter, and it made me smile.

Dancing is, to me, an opportunity to break free of convention and the humdrum life, a chance to revel in what our bodies can do. A celebration. Not everyone dances, but everyone who can, should. It doesn't matter if you look like a "Dancing with the Stars" sensation, or just the neighborhood klutz. God made us to move. But not only that…

Dancing with a partner adds a whole other dimension to the experience. It can be the awkward guy who took you to prom. It can be the love of your life. But the give-and-take of the dance unites the partners in a special moment in time. You occupy the same space, and sway to the same sounds. You are totally in tune with each other, and that is a rare thing.

St. Catherine writes about a God who yearns to dance with us. A God who loves us so utterly that He doesn't care if we aren't Fred Astaire—or even close. He just wants to connect with us, at this special moment in time (which is every moment, glad or sad). To celebrate being alive with us. To be totally in tune with us, just as we are.

So what do you say? Are you willing to cast aside your doubts and fears and inhibitions? The amazing dance floor that is life is right here, waiting for you. The light is perfect, be it sunlight or starlight or spotlight. The music is glorious. Your Partner is sublime.

Step out. Begin. 1-2-3, 1-2-3, 1-2-3. See? You're doing it! You're doing it!

You are waltzing the Heavenly Waltz with your oh-so-loving God.

Dance on.

PROCRASTI-NATION

"Procrastination is the art of keeping up with yesterday."

--Don Marquis

If I spoke Spanish (which I don't) my favorite word would be mañana (tomorrow). I put everything, and I do mean everything, off until later—much, much later. This goes for planning Confirmation class and writing children's sermons (which I've been known to do on the way to church), also grocery shopping (I hold off till the only edible in the refrigerator is ketchup) and laundry (there's a reason we own 312 towels). I've never gone to the doctor or dentist when I should—the way I figure it, no news is good news! The final day to register for a class or program without penalty is the day I do—often at 11:59 PM. And sometimes, I have to pay the penalty—which is galling, but clearly not galling enough for me to change my ways.

You see, I live in the ProcrastiNation, and in our family I have a fair amount of company. The Seyfried motto: It'll wait! Steve can write an entire play in a couple of days, which is good because the first performance is usually only a week away. Sheridan stays in bed until 6:40 and can still catch a 6:47 train (I swear to God, and this includes getting fully dressed and eating something). Evan has vastly improved, thanks to the Naval Academy, but I still remember the quarter-long high school Biology project done in five days (this involved various types of bread and how fast they grew mold, so it was quite the challenge!) Back in the years of her baking business, Rose mastered sticking the hot cookies in the freezer so they cooled fast enough to wrap for a customer who needed them a half-hour earlier. And what can I say about PJ? He is the president of the ProcrastiNation, a man who never orders replacement contact lenses until the last pair (the pair he's wearing) has been in for weeks. Julie is a chip off the Seyfried block, as her fish swims in a bowl full of murk and her room gets so messy she has to sleep upstairs on the sofa.

Sometimes we procrastinate when there's a chance whatever we're supposed to do will just go away. Yard work leaps to mind here...eventually it's winter, and those weeds and unraked leaves disappear under a thick layer of snow. And if we wait to respond to that awkward email long enough, it will fall so far down in the queue that we can, honestly, say we've forgotten all about it.

Sometimes, we're just addicted to the adrenaline rush of delay, the extra spice all those zero-hour saves give to life. Let others start the project on schedule, let others plan ahead. Promptness is for wimps. We need to bump up against the absolute deadline to get the juices flowing!

I hate to admit it, but I am personally a faith procrastinator as well. It's so easy to tell myself I will pray later, read Scripture tomorrow, love my neighbor next week. There will be time, right? I'll get it done, at some future point. Just not today. There's only one little problem with this plan: we none of us are promised tomorrow. We can't afford to put off any opportunities to talk with our God, learn more about Him, show His love to others. Now is all we have for sure. I tell myself this, and I believe it, but it's just so hard to renounce my citizenship in the ProcrastiNation!

Well, I think I just found my Lenten resolution. Traditionally, I make a list of things I vow to do without during this contemplative time (and traditionally I salt said list with things I already hate, to give me a sense of accomplishment). But no giving up stewed cabbage and hang-gliding for me this year! I will seize the day, THIS day, and try to start putting my spiritual house in order. And who knows? Maybe I'll get around to dealing with my unwritten thank you notes, my dusty furniture, and my dish-clogged sink too.

May I finally say, and mean: adios, mañana!

FOR SALE

"Everyone lives by selling something."
--Robert Louis Stevenson

A few months ago I got a phone call. It was a neighbor's son contacting me about a "project" he was working on. Could I give him a few minutes of my time? "Certainly!" I replied. I'm all for imparting some of my wisdom to the younger generation. I imagined a school assignment that required interviewing a person old enough to remember Herman's Hermits and love beads. I'd definitely fill that bill!

Nay! Turned out the lad had a different agenda. He was out to sell me Cutco knives. I flinched, because I've been down that road many times before. My premiere foray into the world of razor sharp kitchen implements was a presentation by a young actor who was working for us, and still, surprisingly, falling short of making a decent living. So he shilled for Cutco. Next came the daughter of a woman I hadn't seen, no joke, in 20 years. She, too, arrived on my doorstep with an assortment of cutlery. More recently, our dear young friend Hannah came a-calling. She had a refreshing attitude: just let me cut some rope in your kitchen, blurt out my spiel, and we can all go back to our lives. Halfway through her Cutco speech, her cell phone rang. It was the offer of a better job! Hannah literally threw her knives in the bag and then and there called it a career.

Now, I am sure Cutco makes a product far superior to anything found in my kitchen drawer. For the record: my knives are old, and not as sharp as they should be (but then, neither am I). But I am emotionally attached to each one of them—paring, chef's, serrated—and have no intention of, or budget for, adding to my little collection. However, Cutco pays the salesperson something for every booking, even if nothing is sold, so why not listen to the kid? I thought.

This encounter brought back many memories from my childhood. My father was a furniture salesman, and not a good one. He made a very modest living selling Danish Modern sofas and tables to stores. We ended up furnishing our various homes with his samples, our living room adorned with chairs of black leather and chrome that you'd need a crowbar to get out of, and Rya rugs so thick that you wanted to mow them. He was on the road throughout the South every single Monday-Friday, each week hoping he would interest a store or two in this very contemporary furniture. In those days the prevalent taste down in Dixieland was for much more traditional stuff, and Dad was not exactly the Great Persuader—that was a bad combination. So, for years I watched him come back from his weekly road trips, tired and defeated. When I grew up, I vowed, I would never sell anything.

Yet here I am, selling myself at every turn. Buy my books! Buy my articles! Book me as a speaker! I loathe this part of the business and wish I could hire someone to take my place. It gets really old. I wish I had a better product to offer. I lack the confidence to pound on doors, to cold-call, to do what I know it takes to successfully hawk wares. It's a hard-knock life, being a salesperson, and I applaud those brave enough to attempt it.

And so the Cutco Kid arrived. He opened his sales kit and showed me how his butcher knife saws through wood. I sat, listening patiently, as I wish others had sat for my dad, long ago.

BUSTING OUT ALL OVER

"But it's comin' by gum/You can feel it come/You can feel it in your heart/You can see it in the ground/You can see it in the trees/You can smell it in the breeze/Look around! Look around! Look around!"
   --Rodgers and Hammerstein, Oklahoma!

June will be busy around here. Evan is due home on leave from Hawaii prior to his Washington, DC reassignment. Vacation Bible School runs the 25th-29th, with our youth mission trip to Queens, NY immediately following. Oh, and did I mention there will be a wedding too?

All of the aforementioned events are causing me stress. In the case of Evan, we—and he— just don't know his exact plans and may not for a while yet (thank you, US Navy!). VBS is always a whirlwind, as 50 little ones descend upon Christ's Lutheran. Why I head up this venture is a mystery, as my ability to do crafts, play games, lead music or decorate the space is just about nonexistent. Thankfully I have lots of handy helpers, but still I fret. Will this be the year a child breaks his leg playing "Parting of the Red Sea"? Will Thursday's snack cause an outbreak of food poisoning? Will one whiny four year old set off a chain reaction of preschool sadness, necessitating a battery of "come and get 'em" calls to parents?

Though our mission trip destination is virtually in our backyard (as opposed to Guatemala, Alaska or Costa Rica), there are still a jillion little details to work out and, as usual, I'm way behind. I haven't rented the minivans yet (mandatory for transporting 17 people, their luggage and air mattresses). Haven't gotten my TB test yet either (mandatory when working with children in New York State). Haven't even learned to parallel park (mandatory when driving in Queens). My skills in this last department bring to mind Woody Allen's line in the movie *Annie Hall* ("It's OK. We can walk to the curb from here.")

But all of this pales in comparison to my panic as I contemplate the impending chiming of wedding bells. It doesn't help that, every single time I mention the nuptial date (June 23) someone asks, "THIS June 23rd?" Yes, THIS June 23rd! I know it's soon! Arrrggghh! There is a ceremony to pull together! There is a reception to plan! There are out-of-towners who must be housed and fed! Annoyingly, there is the engaged couple, who refuse to worry about any of this. They have it under control. What, they wonder, is my problem? And you know what's even more annoying? They DO seem to have things under control.

The happy pair wants to keep everything super simple. They haven't invited a big crowd. They are both music directors of churches, so I'm guessing they might possibly have an idea or two about the music. Ya-Jhu has her dress, and Sheridan promises to iron his shirt. They know what they want for flowers and food, and plan to do much of the work themselves, with help from family and friends. They sail through these pre-wedding weeks serenely, enjoying every moment together. The nerve of them!

The rehearsal dinner will be at our house. It'd be really nice to gut it (the house) and start from scratch, but that is, alas, not an option. So hubby Steve has put together a laughably long "to do" list. This list includes repairing the sliding glass door, buying new curtains (family room and shower), and purchasing a new dishwasher (ours went kaflooey months ago, and my dishpan digits attest to all the plates and bowls and cups I've been hand-washing). Ya-Jhu's parents will be sleeping in PJ's room when they come from Taiwan. At the moment, unless they are mountain goats, they will not be able to navigate the heaps of clothes and books and baseball cards adorning the floor. My sister C will be arriving from Honolulu. What are her sleeping options? Right now, the pen with the bunnies is the likeliest spot for her to snooze. And what about the menu? A cookout is the practical solution, given our small dining room, but what if it rains? And I'm here to tell you, if I am involved, it will rain. When I headed the neighborhood picnic committee, there was a monsoon. When I helped plan the elementary school field day, there was a flash flood. The only ones who love me on these occasions are the ducks.

Have I adequately conveyed the number of things that need attention, the number of things that could go wrong?

I buzz frenziedly around my son and his fiancée, and they probably wish they could swat me. They are the cool and calm center of this maelstrom that is Sheridan and Ya-Jhu's Wedding. They refuse to let me ruin this happy time, and God bless them. They are wisely aware that June 23rd is just one day; the most important thing is what happens June 24th, and every day of their married lives thereafter. Sher and Yaj have a secure handle on what matters most, and it has nothing to do with the cake (will it come out lopsided?) or the wine (Jesus probably won't work His wonders, so will there be enough?) or the tiny flower girl and ring bearer (will their cuteness trump their possible tantrums?) The bride and groom-to-be gaze into each other's eyes, and see a beautiful future there. And, when I stop obsessing for one minute, I gaze at them, two young people I love very much, and know that it really will all come out fine.

So bring it on, June. We'll be ready. I hope.

THE MAGIC PASSPORT

"The world is a book and those who do not travel read only one page."

--Augustine of Hippo

Feeling somewhat Orelandbound this afternoon...you know, the feeling that you are stuck in your little corner of America, making an endless loop of work, grocery store and home—with a trip to the mall a wild-and-crazy adventure. Been awhile since I've left the greater Philly area. Been awhile since I've had my passport stamped.

The Seyfried children all own passports with multiple stamps. They have been to: France, Germany, Italy, Switzerland, the UK, Hungary, Czech Republic, Austria, Netherlands, Estonia, Thailand, Singapore, Japan, Taiwan, Brazil, Uruguay, Peru, Jamaica, Costa Rica, and Guatemala. Though these travels were completely self-funded, the kids know they are still lucky to have had these chances to see so much of the world at such young ages. They may hail from Oreland, but they have never been Orelandbound.

Seyfried Passport Follies include several stories of loss. Sheridan used his passport as basic ID for years (he is still driver's license-less) without incident. Now he has a photo ID, but a few months ago he lost that precious travel book. Luckily he discovered this early enough to re-apply before he and his wife Ya-Jhu were due to take off for their meet-the-relatives trip to Taiwan. When Rose spent a year in Thailand, she put her passport in a wooden box for safe keeping. MUCH to her dismay, when she opened the box, she discovered that the passport had been a snack for hungry Thai termites! Evan was on vacation in South America, and left his passport in a taxicab in Montevideo. God and the taxi driver were good, however, and man and book were swiftly reunited.

PJ is eagerly anticipating his semester abroad next year in Marburg, Germany. Julie, a recent high school graduate, has spent many months working and saving and plotting a grand adventure for the fall. She hopes to go everywhere from Turkey to Finland, visiting international friends along the way. She's planning to travel light, but knows to hold onto that all-important passport for dear life.

I didn't own a passport until I was 43. I'd seen a decent amount of my own country, but none of others (except pre-passport Canada). When I was a child, I'd longed to see the world. An early career ambition of mine had been to become a foreign correspondent for a big city newspaper. But it was, it seemed, not meant to be. No flitting from Paris to Rome getting scoops for me! Instead, my life came to center around my big family, and "travel" became a constant parade of trips to the Acme.

Over time, I convinced myself that I didn't care. My world was pretty small; what of it? After a while, I even started to become fearful of venturing far away from home. I focused on any disturbing news coming from overseas, and mentally circled the wagons. Besides, even if I did go, I would be an easy target for the armies of pickpockets I imagined were everywhere; my every word and gesture would shriek "tourist!" Why take a chance? So there I was, Mom the Stick-in-the-Mud, constantly waving goodbye as my children embarked on so many wonderful trips.

Ultimately, my curiosity trumped my qualms, and the passport was purchased. The travel ground was broken at last by my time in Jamaica in 2000, with Rose and my sister Carolyn. We were only there four days, but it whetted my appetite for more exotic excursions. Not long after that, I went on several mission trips to Central America. My worldview has expanded drastically. I've seen how other folks live, seen some incredible natural wonders, and been the recipient of warm hospitality wherever I've gone. Nary a pickpocket so far! I still would love to go to Europe, Asia and Africa…and now I dare to hope I will live to accomplish my goals.

My advice to the passport-less? Invest in one if you can! The world is out there to be experienced, and it is a crime to be forever Orelandbound (or its equivalent). You truly never know what opportunities may open up for you to travel far, and it's smart to be prepared. My Steve is applying for his first passport soon, and I think it's a wonderful statement of optimism.

This late spring afternoon, I pull out my passport and dream of journeys yet to come, future stamps from Spain and Scotland, Tanzania and Vietnam. I feel hopeful and excited, and a whole lot less Orelandbound.

This afternoon, I wish you the same hope and excitement. Send me a postcard, if you think of it.

WONDERS NEVER CEASE

"Know yourself to improve yourself."
--Auguste Comte

So how do the Seyfrieds bond on the day after Thanksgiving? Traditionally, weather permitting, everyone but me troops out to a state park for a vigorous hike. These adventures (I've seen the photos) involve endless trails through the forest, steep and slippery climbs to scenic overlooks. Traditionally, I stay behind, alone with my leftover pie, and wait to be regaled when my weary, but happy, family returns.

For some reason, last year they convinced me to join them for a trip to Evansburg State Park. Maybe I'd finally had enough pie. Maybe I was just acutely conscious of how rare our time together truly is. In any event, there I was, at trail's beginning, obvious newbie to the rugged outdoor life: pristine white sneakers, too many layers, no water bottle and no clue. My husband had been there before, and confidently led the way. As I huffed and puffed, bringing up the rear, Steve tossed off the fact that we were embarking on a 5 mile, 2 ½ hour "walk." Too late to retreat—I'd never find my way back to the car anyway. So on I marched, until the first slight incline, when I fell. My hope that my stumble would elicit enough pity to cut the hike short then and there, was dashed when PJ just broke off a tree branch and handed it to me as a walking stick. OK, so this is how it was gonna be—no coddling for Mom, the Mom who had given painful birth to these wretched unsympathetic children!

The next two hours plus featured: mud. Mud under fallen leaves, mud hidden beneath the grass, mud right out there in the open. And, of course, mud caked on my formerly pristine white sneakers. It was so bad that Fearless Leader Dad finally caved and let us trek the final mile or so off the trail and on a beautifully dry and civilized paved road. My kind of nature at last! Street signs! Lawns! And, at long last, the parking lot where our car awaited to whisk us home! Home to pie! But also, home, this time, to laugh and remember—all of us, together—our state park adventure.

This Thanksgiving, because of time-crunched schedules, the gang opted to head to the neighborhood park instead of going hiking. Basketball and Frisbee were on the menu. As the others grabbed sneakers and sports gear I, back to my usual routine, prepared to bring a book and sit on a bench while my clan did my exerting for me.

My children's powers of persuasion are considerable, however, and my al fresco reading just wouldn't cut it. Wasn't my 2011 hike enough to satisfy them? No! I had to PARTICIPATE! Mind you, this is a woman who has literally never played either game in her entire life. Basketball was a total mystery to me, and as for Frisbees: whenever and wherever they were flung, I automatically ducked. "Don't worry Mom, none of us are that good," Rose tried to reassure me. But I knew quite well that "not that good" in their universe is "1000% better than me" in mine.

Patience was the watchword as Sheridan showed me—and showed me—and showed me, the wrist flick that would send the Frisbee soaring in the right direction. Turns out, once I stopped ducking, I could actually catch the thing. I just couldn't throw it to save my soul. PJ was a bit of a showoff, catching the disc behind his back, then spinning it clear across a field. Next to him, my attempts to get that #@%%&## Frisbee airborne were totally pathetic. It occurred to me that I'd be better off just walking over and handing it to him. Lo and behold, though, after the jillionth try, I started to get the hang of it.

Giddy from my unexpected success, I proceeded to the basketball court. On the opposite end of the court, Steve and

Evan were playing very intense one-on-one. Back over in the baby pool, so to speak, my only goal was to make one basket. One basket and I'd be thoroughly satisfied.

Well guess what, sports fans? 12, count 'em, 12 baskets! Where is that video camera when you need it? Even as I accomplished this feat I couldn't believe I was doing it. But my aching muscles the next day attested to the fact that the miraculous had indeed happened at the East Oreland playground.

The kids were generous with their praise, and I felt vaguely athletic, just as I'd begun to feel on the trail. However, unless the family REALLY pushes, I'll stick my nose back in my book, eat my pie and let THEM exercise next year. Because it's been unsettling, this late-day discovery that I might not be completely uncoordinated. If I'm not the klutz I always identified myself as, then what other assumptions of mine might be wrong too?

WAITING FOR GODOT IN LOGAN SQUARE

"*Nothing happens. Nobody comes, nobody goes. It's awful.*"
--Samuel Beckett, *Waiting for Godot*

"You seem like an intelligent person. Do you understand what is written on my t-shirt? I got this shirt at St. John's Hospice." The tall, graying, alarmingly thin man spoke with urgency, his piercing blue eyes fixed on mine. Waiting for Godot, the shirt read. I'd seen the play. "Do you get it?" he continued. "We're all waiting. We do things, some of them good things, some of them bad. In the end, it doesn't matter. We're all just waiting. Don't you see?"

An hour earlier, an hour before my encounter with this very intense gentleman, I was driving into town with three of our CLC youth group members. People were waiting for us. They were waiting, roaming around on a patch of grass across from Family Court on the Parkway. We could see them. We had a carful of food and drinks for them. We just couldn't reach them. We had to circle (and circle, and circle) around the Cathedral and still—no legal parking space opened up. There was a fundraising walk by the Art Museum this afternoon, and signs everywhere around proclaiming temporary parking suspensions. We had cases of water bottles and bags and bags of brownies and apples and pretzels...much too much to carry a distance from a lot.

As we made yet another pass at our destination, suddenly, a car pulled out, right in front of the park. We unloaded our

103

cargo and carried everything over to a small table beneath a tree.

The wait was over. Song and worship sheets were distributed. Rainclouds were gathering, but no one seemed in a hurry to rush things along. A high, clear soprano voice led the first hymn, "Leaning on the Everlasting Arms." The congregation sang out, loudly, with enthusiasm. Prayers followed, including the Serenity Prayer, which many seemed to know by heart. A Bible passage from the gospel of Matthew, in which Jesus asked the Pharisees about John the Baptist—whether his baptism came from Heaven or Earth. As I listened, I had a mental image of the wandering John the Baptist. A homeless prophet. I looked out across the lawn and saw his kinsfolk everywhere.

Violet Little pastors this Welcome Church, an extraordinary monthly open-air gathering of some of the marginalized souls of Philadelphia. This afternoon, she shared a story from writer Tony Campolo. Once Campolo helped to organize a party, late at night in a Honolulu diner, for a prostitute who had never in her whole life had her birthday celebrated. The diner owner found out Tony was a preacher and asked what kind of church he belonged to. Tony responded, "I belong to a church that throws birthday parties for prostitutes at 3:30 in the morning."

The message? That is what all churches, and all people, are supposed to do: reach out and celebrate each other and lift each other up and love. Just love. This sermon clearly spoke to the crowd—when were their birthdays last celebrated?

The peace was passed—we all shook hands and told one another our names. Then communion: wafers and grape juice blessed and shared by all. More singing. "This Little Light of Mine." "Amazing Grace."

Now time to distribute coffee and hot chocolate and food—for some, perhaps, their only meal today. People approached in an orderly fashion, waiting patiently. Mallory, Carrie and Nick helped give out sandwiches, packs of goldfish crackers, wool blankets and smiles. My final conversation of the afternoon was with the man with the Godot t-shirt. Again and again, he insisted that we're all just waiting. His life must seem like this, like a bad dream that keeps happening, as he waits for his fortunes to change. Life for the homeless really must feel like the Theatre of the Absurd. What to make of these up-ended expectations? This cloud of addiction, of mental illness? These reversals of fate that sent them from secure jobs and homes out onto the street? Out where they wait in lines for a place to sleep. A meal. For someone to speak words of comfort and caring. They wait.

The group was breaking up now, everyone shuffling slowly away with their blankets and bags of food. Pastor Little gave many hugs, and spoke warm words. These people are not strangers to her, but friends. This outreach is a calling, not an occasional thing but a regular part of her life. It would probably rain soon, rain on these men and women who are exposed to every element. But for this hour, they were all dry, and safe. They had raised their hands and hearts and voices in worship. And, for a few sacred moments, we all felt the loving presence, not of Godot, but of a God who never keeps us waiting.

OF A CERTAIN AGE

"With a long life I will satisfy him and let him see my salvation."

-- Psalm 91:16

Well, folks, it's happened. I got my first senior citizen discount in the supermarket I frequent at the Delaware shore. Shoppers ages 55 and up get a 5% discount every Tuesday. I stood in line with my driver's license, ready to prove I was old enough (it'd been awhile since I'd been carded, but I knew the drill). Much to my chagrin, when I asked for the discount, the (ridiculously young) cashier merely responded "I thought so!" and proceeded to ring up my 5% off without even checking my ID. My measly savings ruined my day, I tell you! Clearly, the people who tell me I don't look my age are liars! Next time, I'll show Superfresh—I WON'T ask for my 5%. So there!!

Age is a funny thing (funny peculiar, not funny ha-ha). When I was in my teens, I yearned for nothing more than adulthood. It drove me crazy when the grownups told me to enjoy my youth. Youth to me meant restrictions, and being belittled. My opinion didn't matter. I was just a kid, after all (even though, in my mind, I had far more sophisticated views on politics, religion, you name it, than my clueless parents). 18 was a triumph, 21 even more so. And so on I flew through my twenties, thirties and forties, blessed with a big smile and a freckled Irish face, and a manic energy level, that erased years just as I began to wish for a little erasure.

I expected that life's ups and downs would tell on me a bit (nothing like birthing five children for retaining toned abs!)

but I didn't count on the wrinkles and how fast they would appear. Good thing my eyes began to give out around then—my morning visage in the mirror became a comforting blur. In my head, and my heart, I was frozen in time, and the time was 1980.

So, I am brought up short by the fact that I am getting old. My earthly span is, by any standard, more than half over (unless I start hanging out with centenarians on a regular basis, which, come to think of it, is a dandy idea. For example, I am the youngest member of my Bible study and it's delightful). My memory is failing rapidly; my reflexes ain't what they used to be. I flake out ridiculously early at night (me, who used to begin her social evenings after 9 PM). I'm the older lady blocking Aisle 6 reading the ingredients on the food labels (when I remember to bring my reading glasses to the store) to make sure whatever it is I may be consuming boosts my "good" cholesterol (whatever that means). Ugh to all of it!

It is a young, young world, where the latest technology is designed (I'm convinced) to confound people of a certain age, and make our landscape a puzzling and disorienting place for those with gray hair. I squirm when I recall my impatience with my folks, especially my mom Joanie. She took computer COURSES, for Lord's sake, and still didn't know what a website was (I asked her for the Today Show's web address and she replied, "30 Rockefeller Center"). There was no hurry in Joanieland. She'd reread the same books over and over again (often tomes about the Kennedys, with whom she was obsessed). She'd be totally content with a trip to the pool and meandering conversations at the water's edge with other seniors. Borrring!! Why couldn't she just keep up, just snap it along?

Well, now she is gone, and I wonder why I hurried her so during her last years. On some level, she knew she was nearing her end on this planet, and was putting the brakes on, to get the most out of her time left. She didn't need a daughter on such an absurdly tight schedule, urging her forward. I'm so sorry, Mom. I deserve to have my kids do the exact same thing to me as my pace slows, even as I pray they will be more patient than I was.

There is an image, often depicted in art (often kitschy art to be sure), of Christ surrounded by kids, holding the sweet cherubs in His lap. "Suffer the little children to come to me," He says. But today, I offer you another image: Christ comforting the aging, His arms around the slightly befuddled gentleman and the arthritic grandma. While children blossom with love, so do the older folks among us—and they are often less likely to receive it. They certainly receive it from Jesus. Why not from me?

As I watch the cashier ring up my discounted order, I realize I'm on the other side of the mountain called life, heading inexorably down. Heading home, to a God who is waiting—patiently—for me someday. May I cherish my elders, soon to be my contemporaries, and let go of my hang up about being young. I'll never be 30 again (or 55, for that matter). Let me continue to challenge myself, physically and mentally, but then give me the grace to slow down. There's nothing wrong with a senior discount. In fact, it's kind of cool.

NO MORE TEARS

"In the terms of "mental illness": Isn't stable a place they put horses that wish to run free?"

--Stanley Victor Paskavich

I'd love to see a grown woman cry. If that woman was me.

In my office at church, I have a box of tissues that I have never touched. Oh, there have been several times over the years when upset parishioners have grabbed a Kleenex or two for mopping up their tears. Never me. I don't cry anymore. Not a drop. Go ahead, make me watch *The Notebook*! I promise you, there won't be so much as a sniffle. My eyes are dry as the Sahara, and I don't see things changing anytime soon.

What has happened to me? Me, who as a little girl would, as my Grandpa often said, cry at card tricks? Me, who as an adult wept buckets over corny TV commercials (remember the Budweiser ad with the Clydesdales pulling a sleigh through the snow to the tune of "I'll Be Home for Christmas"? Killer!) and sad novels and the most minor disappointments of life? And happiness! I cried for joy as well, at every reunion of family or friends, at childbirth (after the baby was born of course—before that it was all blood-curdling shrieks), on giving or receiving gifts of any kind: "Oh, (sob) You shouldn't have!" My face was in a state of permanent blotch from all the waterworks. Before my diagnosis of manic depression, I could literally cry from morning till night—and often did. One memorable New Year's Day I was such a misery that I couldn't stop wailing long enough to join the family for our

111

traditional bowling outing (what's so melancholy about bowling?)

Then, suddenly, my ocean dried up. One day I was blubbering as usual over something sweet one of the kids did; the next, I wasn't able to manufacture a single salty teardrop. And ever since, with everything I've experienced, from happy surprises to tragic turns of events, my body's reaction has basically been: "so what?"

So who turned off the faucet? The answer, as far as I can figure, is pharmaceutical. After many frustrating months of trial and error, my doctor and I found the combination of medications that keep the bipolar disorder under control. Side effects are minimal—no seizures, no weight gain. But I've come to realize that, since the day I began this regimen of drugs six years ago, I haven't shed a tear. Even at loved ones' funerals. I may be "better," but I've lost something I valued greatly…the ability to feel things as deeply as I once did. I mentally skate on the surface of my existence. I am, a lot of the time, pretty numb—as if I'm viewing a not-terribly-engrossing movie about my life, and am tempted to leave the room.

I hate to admit it, but there are many times that I really miss my lows—and my highs as well. Miss the roller coaster of feelings, good and bad. Oh, deep down I still care, but I'm physically unable to show it, and it stinks. Now, I'm never seriously tempted to go off my meds; that would be suicide I know. But I wish, with all my heart, that I hadn't regained my sanity at the expense of my emotions. I wish there was a way to recapture the Elise whose eyes filled at the drop of a hat. I'd love to be, for just one more day, the sobbing lady listening to a bittersweet Billie Holiday song, the mad weeper watching YouTube videos of cute babies, the inconsolable crier sharing a friend's sorrow.

I want to cry again, darn it. And I just can't.

HOME, SWEET HOMESCHOOL

"Living is learning and when kids are living fully and energetically and happily they are learning a lot, even if we don't always know what it is."

--John Holt

For someone who loved learning as much as I did, I wasn't a very happy camper in school. Part of the problem was that we moved around so much; I was ALWAYS the new kid in town, with all the attendant social issues. Part of it surely was my gnat-like attention span, even when I was young. My grades were always good; my spirits, not so much. I remember the all-nighters when I would, start to finish, create my term papers, banging away on the old Royal typewriter. I'd long for the halcyon time ahead when there would be no more chapter tests, no more SATs. As a high school junior, I got my one and only low grade ever, a (gasp!) "D," in an exquisite form of torture known as "Finite Math." Mrs. Carter may as well have been teaching the class in Swahili for all I comprehended. (Note: I am 56. I have never once needed to use finite math—whatever it was, exactly. I forget).

Amazingly, I graduated from St. Pius High with honors (a National Merit Finalist, no less). I went to college at Georgia State University as an engaged, then married, woman. The newlywed/commuter student combo didn't pan out that well for me. I stuck it out for almost three years, then left the hallowed halls of academe to make my fame and fortune (hah!) in the theatre.

Umpty-ump years later, I periodically wonder if I should go back and finish my degree. But clearly, if I wanted to that badly, I would have done it by now. My life is fine (don't cry for me, Argentina!) Still, I sometimes think: would I have fared better as a homeschooler? It wasn't an option I was aware of back in the day. Imagine my surprise when the option presented itself to my children! And several of them said "yes!"

Now there have been three. Three homeschooled teens out of five total kiddos.

Evan and PJ LOVED traditional high school, and thrived there. Indeed, had they chosen to homeschool I cannot say if they—or I—would have survived the experience. Both boys were wont to procrastinate about assignments until zero hour (or beyond). When Evan was in fifth grade, he completely blew off a book report, a diorama affair involving shoeboxes, construction paper and glue. Not only did he not make his diorama, he didn't even bother to read the book. To teach him a lesson, I marched him into class, empty-handed. His golden-hearted teacher, Mrs. Ulrich: "Now, Evan, you didn't do the assignment so I can't give you an A. But if you get it done you can certainly get a B+!" Yay! Lesson learned! Don't bother following directions, you'll always get a second chance! PJ was not much better, skating by with the bare minimum most of the time. It was tough enough mothering these two without attempting to teach them as well.

Sheridan, Rosie and Julie were different. For a variety of reasons, when they were high school juniors they flew the Upper Dublin coop. Sher had music conservatory on his radar screen; to that end he was spending six hours a day composing and practicing—on top of a regular school schedule. Rosie was in Thailand as a junior, and returned to the States a different person—or at least, not a person thrilled by pep rallies and locker decorating. Julie was restless, dreaming of travel and work and more of an independent life. In each case, we agreed to pull them out of school for home education.

It's been quite a ride. All three youngsters had a plan, and it really fell to Steve and me to get out of their way and let them go for it. Sheridan wrote some terrific papers and aced

Algebra II. Rose took Astronomy at community college. Julie used her trips to London, Guatemala and Hawaii as inspiration for essays, photo journal and poetry. I feel silly accepting praise for teaching them—they really taught themselves. In addition, it was a total joy to have them around during the day. Julie and I have gotten some great walks in; Rose and I enjoyed coffee dates; I loved my sneak peek at Sher's new pieces.

Today I accompanied Jules for her annual portfolio review. Her homeschool evaluator looked over all of her year's paperwork and pronounced it complete. Now it will go to the school district for another examination. Julie is bubbling over with plans for her senior year—a trip overseas, 25 books to read. If her experience is like her sibs', she'll get into a good college with no problem.

However they've been schooled, my kids are on their way. Responding to learning in their own styles. One by one on the launch pad, eager to jump into the rest of their lives.

LIFE WITH STEVO

"Let the wife make the husband glad to come home, and let him make her sorry to see him leave."

--Martin Luther

Steve and I recently celebrated our 36th wedding anniversary. Little known fact: I got married at age four. Seriously, though, it's been a long and mostly happy haul, with the requisite ups and downs, made so much more meaningful with our raft of children. I swore I would be a "normal" parent—always loving and giving, never embarrassing. And yet, I am the poster child for "abnormal" a lot of the time, and have mortified my offspring on many an occasion I'm sure. Steve would probably say the same. My weirdnesses could fill a book (and have—three of them in fact). For the record, here's a glimpse of Steve's.

Our Julie recently found (and posted on Facebook) an absolutely hilarious YouTube video of a baby falling asleep sitting bolt upright. The infant would nod off, head would drop drop drop then UP it would go, eyes would open, awake again...but in a second sleep would overtake him once more. Julie's caption? "Dad as a baby." I got a charge out of Julie's affectionate teasing, and Steve did too.

We're quite used to Dad dropping off this way, so exhausted is he by his ridiculous schedule. He swears he is adequately rested, yet how can he be with a 4 AM awakening? He goes downstairs, on to a day that includes officework, teaching an after-school class, a rehearsal and often one or two performances. No wonder he's off to Dreamland the minute he hits the sofa at night (or earlier். His shins emerge bruised after every dinner party from my kicking him back to consciousness under the table).

The children are also used to a father who often wears dresses—in his children's shows, I hasten to add. He is an unattractive but fabulously funny Delmarva the wicked stepsister in *Cinderella*, Glinda the Good Witch in *The Wizard of Oz*. His shows, almost 30 in all, are so beloved by our offspring that they can—and do—quote chapter and verse. They've been discussing getting a sibling tattoo (we shall see), and have tentatively chosen the line "No, that's definitely an arm," (from his production of *Robin Hood*—you had to be there) which they plan to have inked on body parts OTHER than their arms. They have, to a person, inherited Steve's great—and goofy—sense of humor.

Another area where Dad comes in for a ribbing: his musical pursuits. What he may lack in talent, he more than makes up in verve and persistence. His repertoire begins with The Kingston Trio and ends with Peter, Paul and Mary—and just a few selections from both. There are times I fervently wish I'd thought to hide the guitar as I hear the unmistakable chords of "Charlie and the MTA" for the umpteenth time. He'll master that tricky tune, by gum, or die trying!

Steve is Master of the Catchphrase. Every male he addresses is "bud," every female, "kiddo." He begins nearly every explanation with "here's the deal." He has grown a wee bit hard of hearing, and gets rather testy when two people are talking at once ("One at a time! One at a time!") I always have to proofread his press releases and website blurbs, just to weed out the multitudinous repetitions of "fast-paced," "sparkling" and "dynamic."

Beyond his signature words and phrases, Steve has a, shall we say, "colorful" vocabulary. It has never been directed at any of us, but is a regular feature of his interactions with inanimate objects—computer, copier, printer, car. Most of his comments are not fit for a G-rated essay, but when he's at his very angriest, what emerges from his mouth is not another profanity but: "You dirty dog!!"—clearly, the ultimate epithet. We tease him about this too.

We also give him a hard time about his propensity for leaving the house and returning almost right away to retrieve forgotten items—keys, phone, briefcase. Indeed, when Sheridan was only about four, he had a comedy routine of coming in, slamming the door, running out, coming in, etc. saying "I'm bein' Daddy."

All kidding aside, his kids adore him, and so do I. They have the utmost respect for his tremendous work ethic, his loyalty, and his love for them, and I know they will always remember those things about their father. I believe they will also remember the laughter that rings through our house, thanks in large part to their goofy, tired, wonderful dad—the ultimate good sport.

So here's to 36 more, Stevo. You're the best.

DREAM A LITTLE DREAM

"I'm sick of following my dreams. I'm just going to ask them where they're goin', and hook up with them later."

--Mitch Hedberg

Why I don't watch horror movies or read creepy books: nothing can top my nightmares for terrifying. I can honestly say that I have never, as far as I can remember, had a happy dream. Even as a small child, I dreamed I went to take my baby sister C out of her crib in the morning—and I lifted her right off her legs. When I was pregnant with Sheridan, I had a vivid dream. I had the baby, brought him home, and he was really little (I mean like three inches long). Later in the dream, I accidentally vacuumed him up off the floor. Imagine my relief when Mr. 7 lbs. 10 oz. came along a few months later—not a chance of him landing in a Bissell bag!

Since the deaths of three close family members (my parents and sister), I dream about each of them at least four or five times a week. They are always in some kind of danger, and I am powerless to help them. In my sister Mo's case, she is usually drowning and I am trying—and failing—to rescue her. Now there's a recipe for blissful slumbers!

Or else I dream I am going somewhere important that involves climbing a steep ladder (I'm wearing high heels, and the ladder is covered with ice) or crossing a rickety bridge over a very deep chasm. Here, my anxiety about not getting where I'm going in time is compounded by my intense fear of heights.

What do all these dire nocturnal imaginings have in common? Me, of course. It's as if all my worries and phobias decided they can't be contained in my waking hours, so they have to run rampant from midnight to dawn.

Over the years I've tried listening to soothing music, reading funny books before bed, leaving a light burning—nothing really helps. Most mornings I awake exhausted, feeling I've been fighting the forces of evil all night. It's a heckuva way to begin a new day.

When the children were small, they all had their bad dreams. We'd go through stretches when we'd often awaken to the uncomfortable feeling of being watched in the dark, only to switch on the light and find a trembling tiny person, ready to dive under the covers with us. The after-hours issues could usually be traced to the more intense moments of Disney films recently viewed (portions of *The Lion King* still creep me out), or bowls of Cocoa Puffs consumed just before bed.

But the only one who seemed to really tap into my special vein of misery was Evan. He had night terrors from the age of nine months on. He'd scream, "Mommy!!" I'd come in to soothe him, and he'd back away as if I were a monster. "NO!!! I want Mommy!!" He was also our sleepwalker; many's the midnight we'd find his bed empty, and go exploring. He'd eventually be located, huddled on a living room chair, or even on the floor. Waking him was extremely tricky, because he'd be so upset and disoriented. Even as I calmed and rocked him, I'd think: the apple doesn't fall far from the tree, poor little thing.

Haven't asked my offspring about their dreams lately. I'd love to picture them snoozing peacefully, rainbows and butterflies dancing in their heads. But deep down I know better. Their probably tortured sleep is my unintended gift that keeps on giving. You're welcome, kids!

So what do these REM experiences mean? Are they Freudian subconscious desires? Who in their right mind would desire such crazy night visitors? Are they, as the Bible often chronicles, messages from God? In which case, dear Lord, please send me an email instead. I swear I'll pay attention. For tonight, just let me sleep!

Oh well. It's getting late. Steve has been dozing for quite awhile, and the house is completely still. My bed beckons me, and, in spite of myself, my eyes are closing. Off to the rickety bridge, off to the perilous ocean in my head. Here we go again.

LEGACY

"We have an infinite ability to make an impact but we have a finite time here to make a difference and to leave some sort of legacy."

--Thomas Narofsky

Wow, it's 2014. Can you believe it? I certainly can't. New Year's comes right after my December 22nd birthday, so I have to simultaneously get used to new numbers for me (gasp! 57!) and for the world. My birthday/New Year's ritual involves both wildly impractical resolutions (learn ancient Greek! Practice hatha yoga!) and reflection (am I where I hoped to be in my life by now? If not, how can I get there, quickly and painlessly?) My introspection often extends to contemplating my inevitable demise. I don't, of course, know the when and how, but I do have control over some parts of the process. For example, I think I have nailed my final wishes.

OK, so I won't have a tombstone. I'm good with that. My sister Mo has a grave in Atlanta, and we rarely get a chance to visit it. I'd like to be donated to science, though I fully expect science to say: "Thanks, but no thanks. Your body is incredibly uninteresting. No need to investigate whatever you happened to die from." So then I will be incinerated and made mulch of, or scattered out to sea. My dad was cremated, and one of our family stories was the jaunt on a boat out into Delaware Bay with Tom's cremains. Little Evan insisted on accompanying us. It was a windy day. As we prayed and scattered, the breeze picked up and literally flung bits of Grandpa into Ev's face. Evan was unaware of it at the time, and we sure weren't going to tell him. He knows now, of course, about his ashy baptism, and we laugh about it.

I have my funeral pretty much planned out. Sher and Yaj will (through their blinding grief of course) compose a gorgeous string quartet. Evan will play Copland's "The Resting Place on the Hill." Rose will sing whatever she wants, because her voice is so beautiful that it won't really matter. "Give Me Jesus" will factor in. PJ and Julie will deliver clever but heartfelt tributes. Boy, I wish I could be there!

I've been thinking lately. What is my legacy? What will I leave my little corner of the world once I shuffle off this mortal coil?

A body of writing, for one thing. Good or bad, I have been relatively prolific over the years. My target audience for it all? Now that I think of it, it's really largely been my kids. I've painted a picture of my life in words in hopes that they will come to understand their neurotic, insecure, but very well-meaning mom.

What else? My small part in "raising" an amazing group of young people from Christ's Lutheran Church–people of great compassion and enthusiasm for doing God's work in the world. I have been so lucky to be one of their mentors for the past 11 years, and I celebrate their dedication and accomplishments and big, big hearts.

Finally, I will leave the world my most precious treasure: my children. I am incredibly proud of each one of them, and have been so so blessed to be their mother. They will live on (God willing) long past my last breath, to gift the universe with their talents. I wish with all my heart I could afford to leave them more of the things that money can buy. I pray that they will be content with the things money can't, foremost of which is my everlasting love for them.

Believe me, I am in no big hurry for my swan song, and hope I have many years left on earth. But if I died tomorrow, I would be very glad to know that there is a small legacy after all.

LET THE GAMES BEGIN

"Fourth is the worst position."
--Sarah Groff, USA triathalon athlete

Confession: I want to be Missy Franklin.
I want to smile adorably as I shatter a world record.
I want to mouth the words to "The Star Spangled Banner" at the ceremony where I will receive my gold medal.
Heck, I'd be happy with the bronze.
Instead, I am, perennially, #4 (or lower). The wannabe, the also-ran. Not quite good enough to win, or even to place, even though I qualified for the team of life.
On vacation in Rehoboth Beach, my newspaper of choice is *The Washington Post*. It is part of the "getaway" experience to read different viewpoints, and considering Rehoboth is billed as The Nation's Summer Capital, I am only one of many who are thumbing through the Sunday *Post* on the sand.
At any rate, an article in today's issue caught my eye. It explored the plight of the Olympians who placed fourth—or worse—in this year's London competition. These dedicated and devoted swimmers, gymnasts, runners...most of them have worked and trained as hard as the medalists, yet still, at the critical moment, fell short. No platform ceremony for them, no celebrity endorsement for Wheaties. Their dreams are shattered, in front of an audience of many millions (something that should only happen in nightmares). They will go home to China and Russia and Cleveland as mere footnotes to the Olympic story. Some will redouble their efforts to qualify for 2016. More will become coaches, or abandon the sports altogether for another livelihood. Life will go on, and many of these men and women will have other triumphs as the

years pass. But the disappointment of a poor performance in the Games will hover like a cloud for quite a while. And we, the fickle public, will be no help. After all, we'll remember Phelps and Williams. Who, besides their loved ones, will recall Khatuna Lorig (archery) or James Carter (track)?

The Olympics is only one prominent example of the drama of winner/loser that is played out in many facets of life. Politics is clearly another major arena where some triumph and others fall by the wayside. Society loves the victorious ones, casting everyone else aside like yesterday's trash.

Glued to the happenings in London on TV, today I find myself rooting for the sure-to-fail. Finisher #4 and below. Rooting for them, not to score a stunning upset perhaps, but to pick themselves up, head high, and go on, no matter what the result. I identify with them, and Jesus does too. Not to take anything away from the Gold, Silver and Bronze recipients...they will have their accolades and deservedly so. But one of the great, great comforts of my faith is my firm belief that God roots for me, whatever the outcome of my contest. He roots for you, too, and doesn't keep score as the world does. CEO or minimum-wage worker, PhD or GED, doesn't matter. He sits in the stands and lets us play. He doesn't interfere but He doesn't miss a trick. His criteria: did we give it our best shot? Did we hang back to help a teammate who stumbled? He searches our hearts for signs of love, and rejoices to find them. We are the Lord's winners, we back-of-the-pack lot.

I don't anticipate a slate of new TV shows titled *Pretty Good Chef, America's Got a Bit of Talent, Almost a Survivor*. We will always be dazzled by the crème de la crème, the top of the line. What matters is, what we value here on earth may not matter in the end.

I want to be Missy Franklin, but I am not. I am Elise Seyfried, flawed and fallible. But just as Missy is, I am a child of God. And what parent isn't proud?

And so, as the 2012 Olympics unfold, I wave my banner high.

Go world. All of us.

ACCENTUATING IT

"Are you afraid someone will think you're American if you speak openly?"

--Lord Grantham, Downton Abbey

It takes me a little while to hop on the bandwagon. By the time I do, everyone else has jumped off and hopped onto the next bandwagon. It is this way with food (broccoli rabe), fashion (ballet flats), technology (iPhone: iFinally got one) and popular culture. My hot new singer is on his third album and other music lovers have moved along to someone who genuinely is at the dawn of a career.

So it is perhaps no surprise that I am only just now getting around to the TV series *Downton Abbey*. Daughters Julie and Rose, and myself, had a catch-up marathon recently, during which we watched all of Seasons One and Two. Season Three is next on our must-see list, and we can't wait. Originally skeptical of the show's power to fascinate, we are now rabid fans of the Granthams and their platoon of servants. Never mind that it is a glorified and gussied-up soap opera! We love Lady Mary and her Matthew (upstairs), Mr. Bates and his Anna (downstairs), etc.

Most of all we love those British accents. They make the speakers sound intelligent and witty, no matter the content of their conversation. To my mind, anyone from the U.K. can recite the phone book (remember them?) and be positively spellbinding. I am a total sucker for foreign accents of any kind. I hear "oui" or "ciao" and I immediately think: mysterious and fascinating, a Person with a Capital P Past. Never mind that that Past may have included a snooze-worthy job and ho-hum family life...for me, speak with an exotic flair and you are a superstar, or a superspy—a super something, anyway.

My globe-trotting offspring have made friends everywhere, from dozens of countries. I envy them their familiarity with the world's citizens. I'm sure these folks have differences—tall, short, blonde, Asian and so on—but I'm equally sure they all SOUND amazing. During Julie's first two weeks in Italy, she has met young people from Scotland, Turkey, Japan and Sweden, all backpacking around Europe. I'd love to see them someday. More than that, I'd love to hear them.

Now, I may be wrong, but somehow I don't believe our various American dialects have the same romantic appeal overseas. For example, I am a native "New Yawkuh," and my husband Steve hails from Indiana, where "pin" and "pen" sound exactly the same. As actors, Steve and I worked hard to rid ourselves of all vocal traces of the lower East Side of Manhattan and Bradbury St. in Indianapolis. We achieved only partial success, and still lapse into the not-so-mellifluous sounds of our youth. Some accents are charming. Our accents are just kind of annoying.

And I'm not too thrilled by the speaking voices of my fellow countrymen either. The South is a hotbed of various speech patterns, from flat (Arkansas) to the *Gone with the Wind* drawl (Georgia), but again, I just don't think "y'all" evokes intrigue; rather, it evokes an image of grits and gravy. My brother-in-law Rob is from "Minnesohda," and when I listen to him I'm smack dab in the middle of *A Prairie Home Companion*. His is a sturdy and stoic parlance typical of one who used to shovel several tons of snow out of his driveway annually.

Perhaps familiarity breeds boredom, and our international counterparts love the way we talk just because it is so different. It may well be that Jacques in Paris finds *parler en Français* très dull, but he would delight in a good ol' Texas twang. Maybe Elly Mae Clampett would have a full dance card if she ventured across the pond. But I rather doubt it.

I'm proud to be an American. I just wish we sounded cooler. Ah well. *C'est la vie!*

SPORTS NUT (NOT)

"I hate all sports as rabidly as a person who likes sports hates common sense."

--H. L. Mencken

Sports spectating is not, as they say, my bag. Living in a city (Philadelphia) known for its sports nuts, I watch with detached amusement as grown men scream and jump up and down, curse, high five each other and spill beer on themselves as they view their Flyers or Sixers or Phillies or Eagles. Who cares? Well, my husband, for one. We have a photo, taken in 1986, of us with 1980 World Series pitcher Tug McGraw (Tug had his own segment on Action News in those days and was covering Steve's children's theatre performance at a school). Steve was thrilled. I was unthrilled in the extreme. Nice guy, Tug was, but what was the big deal?

If I care not a whit for professionals who play the games, you can imagine my keen lack of interest in sports when my own children played. None of them were exactly kindergarten standouts, so what I recall most were the baseball games that lasted well into the night (on unlit fields I might add), when the frenzied dad-coaches swore they could still see the ball and we could go one more inning. I also remember the Arctic chill of late-fall evening soccer. When "our" team was behind, I secretly hoped our opponents would crush us quickly so we could all go home. Confession: during an early Rose basketball game, I was totally engrossed in conversation with my friend Holly. At one point the ref, who happened to be a friend from church, actually came over to me and informed me that Rosie had just made a basket (her very first, in fact), and

133

that I should pretend later to have seen it. I gave an Oscar-worthy performance at halftime, oohing and aahing at her athletic prowess. Knowing Rose, she probably wasn't fooled for a minute, but she gave me the benefit of the doubt.

I kept thinking that my attitude would improve as they grew older. Surely a middle-school baseball tournament, with Sheridan on the pitcher's mound, would be more engrossing than watching the same child at age five, whaling vainly away at T-ball, would have been! Surely I would be swept up in the excitement of the other Upper Dublin High football spectators when PJ took to the field as place-kicker! Nah. Still totally disinterested, still waiting impatiently until the final whistle blew, until the last out was called. I viewed watching my kids' games as my motherly cross to bear, and counted the days until I would be off the hook forever.

Well, guess what? It's happened. I am no longer contractually obligated to sit on any bleachers, anywhere. And you know what? I kinda miss it. Not the sports themselves of course—nor the sports-crazed parents (one parent of a boy on Evan's team was given to shrieking at the children, even following them out to the parking lot afterward to rant and rave). I do, however, miss being an important game-watcher—important to my kids, that is—even when I was rooting for a field hockey player I could have sworn was Julie and wasn't. My offspring never got mad if I cheered their adversary's goal by accident; they just wanted me physically present for them.

So our college man PJ came home for Steve's birthday last April and needed to go back to Millersville University for a lacrosse game (the team he played on was doing very well, on its way to a national championship). On an impulse Steve and I decided to drive out and watch his game. It was all so uncomfortably familiar—the bitter cold, the hard bleachers, the requisite bizarre screaming fan (this guy wore a full yellow bodysuit). But attending PJ's game gave me another chance, maybe one of my last chances ever, to stand up and cheer for my child at play. The years are flying by at a ridiculous pace, and—there's no getting around it—my brood is all grown up. Someday soon, it will be their turn to stand on the sidelines and watch their own offspring score that basket, or (if they take after their Grandma) miss hitting that T-ball. Meanwhile, though, I could still watch PJ (it WAS PJ, wasn't it?) racing down the field.

Wonder of wonders, I enjoyed myself that evening. College lacrosse is, I must admit, very fast-moving and, I guess, even a little bit exciting. PJ was, himself, fast-moving and fun to watch. But best of all: PJ was genuinely happy we had come. And just because of that, I was happy too.

I may still be an ignorant numbskull when it comes to understanding even the rudiments of sport, and I still wouldn't pay ten cents for tickets to anything at Citizen's Bank Park or the Wells Fargo Center. But as long as my kids are glad to see me, anytime, anywhere, I'll be there.

FAKING IT

"We are what we repeatedly do."

--Aristotle

I am just about totally unqualified for anything I do in this world. As a child, I taught myself to read, to cook, to type (with two fingers, the ridiculous method I still use). I received no formal training in writing, acting, or church work. I married my first boyfriend at age 20, with no experience whatsoever in being out on my own. And parenting? Forget about it! I remember the many bouts of postpartum weeping (me and the babies) as I frantically tore through my copies of Dr. Spock and Penelope Leach for advice. That the kids turned out well is a miracle for which I can take very little credit.

For so many years, I plastered a big smile on my face and faked my way through life, ignoring physical ailments and mental illness alike as I pretended to have it all figured out. Even now, at age 57, when you'd think I'd know better, I am still a master of disguise. Ask my psychiatrist how I'm feeling on my current dosage of meds. He will probably say I'm doing great, when in reality I hate my numbness and lack of emotions. Heck, I recently walked around for four months with a torn rotator cuff and denied the pain!

There is value to faking it sometimes, I believe. Steve's dad used to say that when people asked him how he was he always answered "fine" because that's what everyone wanted to hear. We all have our miseries; do we really need to bring each other down by complaining about them? And I have definitely experienced times when the false impression I've given of being happy has eventually morphed into the real thing.

So now here I am, with a new role to play—that of grandma. I am genuinely thrilled for Ya-Jhu and Sheridan, and it is a joy to see how tenderly they care for little Aiden. I feel excited and a bit scared about this new little one who has come into the world. I never prepared myself for grandparenthood at all, and once again felt as if I was faking it, at least at first. Am I being helpful? Hopefully. Am I spoiling the baby? Probably. Will I have the energy to really participate in his daily life in a positive way? Who knows, but I will definitely give it my best shot.

And if someday my precious grandchild asks me for advice about living, I will say that we none of us are ever really prepared, ever feel truly adequate for all of life's challenges. Even when we have a lot more training than I had. I think it's a secret we all carry inside of us: that we're pretending every day. Smiling when we don't feel like smiling. We need to keep on keeping on through the tough times, and fake it till we make it. Because God knows we're trying, every one of us. And maybe trying is the best any of us can do.

THE PLEASURE OF THEIR COMPANY

"When they had gone ashore, they saw a charcoal fire there, with fish on it, and bread...Jesus said to them, 'Come and have breakfast.'"

--John 21:9,12

Had a lovely Easter dinner at our friend Mary Ellen's yesterday. Her son Tim (Evan's good friend) was home, and Mary Ellen was gracious enough to invite all available Seyfrieds (PJ, Julie, Sheridan and our Seyfried-to-be Ya-Jhu). As we ate, I was struck by how very much I enjoy hearing these grown-up kids converse. They moved from Freud and Jung to Lenin and Stalin, and the talk was informative and entertaining. As PJ translated Sheridan's German joke, as Tim talked about his DC job, and as Julie shared funny tales of her brunch shift at the retirement home, I was in Heaven. I had been similarly transported to my happy place when we ate our traditional pre-Christmas Eve supper at Mike and Holly Carlson's. All of both families had gathered for that one—and once again, the patter and laughter flowed freely.

Who are these delightful young people? What has become of our querulous, sloppy, picky children?

Wasn't it just last week that Sheridan was in his high chair, consuming his vat of Gerber oatmeal? He LOVED that stuff, and accompanied every bite with "yum, yum, yum." As he was our first, I thought all babies so vocalized—until we had houseguests who found his sound effects strange and hilarious. Wiry little Evan was far more interested in climbing the dining room door jamb than sitting and consuming anything on his plate. Rosie was a fourth grade vegetarian, a fine choice had she liked any vegetables (a better term for her dietary predeliction: bread-and-cake-arian). PJ sent his drinks flying with such regularity that toddler Julie would automatically head for the kitchen to get a mop-up dishtowel (PJ's New Year's resolution one year: "no more spilling!"—which he kept for about a week). Jules would try any food, but had a hands-down favorite: shrimp alfredo made with—important—canned alfredo sauce. One year I did a from-scratch sauce and she could tell instantly (more preservatives, please!)

Conversationally, my kids were not exactly the Kennedys at the dinner table. The two older boys, in particular, were incredibly unforthcoming about their days at school. When asked, the stock reply was "nothing happened." Apparently, the fire that broke out in the cafeteria one lunchtime also qualified as "nothing" (I heard about it from the mother of a girl, of course). Rosie was a chatterbox, but also incredibly over-sensitive to anything resembling teasing (in addition to a knife and fork, she needed a box of tissues at her place). Often, our dinner convos degenerated into warnings ("PJ, if you keep tipping that chair back you're going to...I TOLD you you would fall!") and fights over the dishes (though we had a chore list, it was apparently never anyone's turn to do them).

One of the things I wonder about the long, silent Biblical stretch concerning Jesus' boyhood: what was mealtime like *chez* Mary and Joseph? Did Jesus and his siblings ever bicker? Did the little Lord practice his miracle-working and convert unleavened bread to honey-cakes? Considering how important dining was during his adult ministry, ranging from meals with friends and Pharisees, to the Last Supper, and the amazing post-Resurrection fish fry on the beach—wouldn't it make sense that eating was an important, even sacred, daily event for the child God? And, given that He was human as well as divine, wouldn't it make sense that some dinnertimes were less than stellar? It comforts me to think of His mom, sighing as she mopped up yet another tabletop mess. I've been there, Mary. I know how you felt. And yet, I am quite sure that there were extraordinary nights when young Jesus revealed His infinite wisdom and love to His family, just as He later would to the world. Those were the nights when all the trouble to set a meal before the children was worthwhile.

In my own (definitely non-holy) way, I have experienced extraordinary evenings too, with my precious brood gathered to eat and talk and laugh together, and I am so grateful. Somehow we have gotten through the years when mealtime was a five-ring circus, and suddenly they've all come out the other side of childhood. Their company, in any combination— and I include their wonderful friends— truly is a pleasure.

Most nights now, the gang is elsewhere, teaching late music lessons downtown, sampling Washington and NYC restaurants, grabbing a fast-food bite at college. I understand, even as I feel a pang removing the extra place settings from the table. I understand. But my invitation is ALWAYS open.

Come on home for dinner, kids. Anytime. I miss you.

NEVER TOO LATE

"Lent comes providentially to reawaken us, to shake us from our lethargy."

-- Pope Francis

Lent starts with Ash Wednesday this week, March 5th. That means Easter is April 20th, about as late as it can possibly be. Daylight Savings Time begins on Sunday, and by Holy Week we will be in the heart of spring, flowers and robins and all. And it has me quite unsettled.

You see, Lent was supposed to be my gloom-and-doom season, when I examined my (guilty) conscience and fretted over my (innumerable) sins. As a Catholic child, I was encouraged to give something up each Lent, something I really enjoyed, like TV or Coke. So skipping the ice cream and Pop Tarts for six weeks just added to the general misery.

My sister Maureen was in the cafeteria at Epiphany School in September of her first grade year. The cafeteria ladies were brutal—no recess until everything on your tray was eaten. As her classmates finished and went outside, poor little Mo remained, glumly contemplating the slimy stewed prunes on her plate. As the time ticked by, she couldn't swallow a spoonful. Finally, inspiration struck. When the cafeteria worker commented on her uneaten prunes, Mo smiled and said, "Oh I'd LOVE to eat my prunes, but I can't. You see, I've given them up for Lent!" When Mrs. Lunch Lady stopped laughing, she allowed Mo to leave her prunes and go out to play.

When I grew older, I stopped giving up (it was kind of absurd; I'd give up desserts, honestly, just to lose five pounds), and started giving more more more...more volunteering, more praying, more general good deeds. And that was better, but I still had the nagging feeling that my positive actions were kind of selfish at root ("Look at me, God! I'm really super duper, aren't I?")

So I settled into a mood of mild depression, as I felt befit the 40 days. The nasty winter weather helped my blues along, with bitter cold and early darkness. But this year! How will I be able to stay "down"? The elusive sun will be shining again, and all around me will be signs of new life. Wait—that's not supposed to happen till Easter at the earliest! Who ever heard of a Happy Lent?

But maybe...

God never meant for us to spend Lent in a funk. Maybe it would be better passed with a sense of peace and hope and, yes, even joy. After all, to dwell only on the sadness of Jesus' death, to beat ourselves up over our faults and scramble madly to win God's favor is to miss the whole point. The point is to recognize Christ's amazing life and His resurrection promise. The point is that God loves us, just as we are, and we can grow to be our best selves because of that grace-filled love.

I believe we can relax about the Ben and Jerry's and the Tote Board of Super Duper Deeds. I believe we can welcome a late Lent this year, and enjoy every beautiful day of it.

ANGELS AMONG US

"Then I saw another angel flying in midheaven, with an eternal gospel to proclaim to those who dwell on earth, to every nation and tribe and tongue and people."

--Revelation 14:6

19 years ago this month, I was at Pennsylvania Hospital awaiting the birth of Bouncing Baby Seyfried #5. Labor wasn't progressing, even after hours of walking in Center City in the bitter early December cold. Back in Oreland, my mom was amusing the other kids with a guessing game— boy or girl this time? While I badly wanted a sister for Rosie, with three boys already, I was prepared for another son. Which would have been fine, had Steve and I been able to agree on a name. I thought the name Charlie was adorable; Steve wasn't so sure. His choice was Benedict, the name of one of his good friends in seminary. I was adamantly against this one (though I liked Ben himself), thinking only of probable nicknames for the poor little guy (Arnold! Eggs!) We had nearly arrived at a compromise monicker, Quinn, but were debating still when we decided to head home. Little Whatshisname was clearly not about to make an appearance today.

But as we cut through the hospital lobby en route to the parking lot, we bumped into the nurse who'd been there when I was first examined in the morning. She took one look at me and said, "You really should go back upstairs and be examined again." She sounded so emphatic that we obeyed. And thank God we did, because that exam revealed the baby's heart rate was dangerously low. By the time I got settled in a room, full

145

labor had kicked in and I was in agony. I don't want to think of what would've happened if we'd been on the Schuylkill Expressway at that moment.

After a tumultuous evening, during which the baby's heart rate fluctuated wildly by the minute, and the decision was finally made to do a Caesarian section, shortly after 1 AM, Julie Claire arrived, safe and sound. We never saw the nurse again, but ever since, we've thought of her as an angel, put into our path to make sure our precious child was OK.

I was thinking of Julie and angels again recently, as she finally came home from her three month backpacking odyssey in Europe. I was so proud of her for attempting this feat, but worried all day, every day about her safety as she traveled through 11 countries alone. With only two minor negative incidents (infected tonsils in Vienna and bedbugs in Nice) throughout the whole trip, and many, many incidents of kind strangers who became friends, I concluded that Jules had an angel on her shoulder, making sure she was OK. Then I realized that these new friends WERE her angels, making her traveling world a safer and happier place.

Do you believe in angels? Heavenly protectors who make sure we're OK? It's hard to square that, isn't it, with the many, many people who suffer hardships, some beyond imagining? Where are their winged advocates? I don't know. But I will say that I believe we have the power to be angels for each other on this bumpy road called Life. Offering a helping hand, an encouraging word. A little love. We can do this.

Welcome home, my Julie. May you always be surrounded by angels, as you are an angel to me.

ZEN AND THE ART OF BABY HOLDING

"For fast-acting relief try slowing down."
--Lily Tomlin

It's hard to imagine me sitting still for two hours, "doing" nothing. But the other afternoon, I did just that. Sat completely still, holding my newborn grandson.

Aiden Jacob, in his two short weeks with us, has turned our household upside down. 24/7, we are aware that there is a baby on the premises. We speak in hushed tones, and turn the sound down on the TV, lest we disturb his (occasional) slumbers. Our arms are ever ready to cuddle and rock him. We are always listening for him to start fussing, and his infant screaming brings me right back to my life circa 1984, when Aiden's father had me on the same high alert.

Our little guy has been a trouper, handling being held by a parade of adoring family members and friends with equanimity. But there are many times when no one but mommy Ya-Jhu will do. We are trying to give her as many breaks as we can, but as a nursing mother she is constantly on call. In short, it is happy chaos around here these days.

I was never much of a meditator. During my one and only yoga class years ago, I groaned my way through the various poses, counting the minutes until we could bow and say "Namaste" (I bow to the Divine Spirit in you) to each other. That was my signal to grab my bag and hightail it to the parking lot, where I would rapidly lose my bliss merging into the rush hour traffic.

Over the years, I have visited Buddhist temples and Quaker meetinghouses, where I have alternately chanted and keep utterly silent, waiting for the magical calming of my mind and spirit these faith traditions offer. No dice. Those were the moments my wayward brain would play "We Are the Champions" on repeat, and my thoughts would drift to whether I had remembered to pull the fish out of the freezer for dinner. When it came to "being there," I usually bombed.

So why did I feel so "there" that day? Because I held my grandbaby, and there was absolutely nothing else I could do. Didn't try to read a book, eat or drink, use the computer. I held Aiden, and time stood still. His furrowed brow (what was he dreaming about?) his impossibly small fingers with their miniscule nails, his intoxicating smell—all completely captivated his Nana. I held Aiden, and 5:30 PM became 7:30 PM in the blink of an eye. I noticed ephemeral things: the heaving of his little chest as he breathed, the breeze floating in through the screen door, the birdsong fading into cricket call as dusk began to replace day. His soft, warm body, so innocent and trusting, curled into mine, and I was as utterly content as he seemed to be.

It took holding this precious baby to make me stop and pay attention to the beauty of life. So thank you, tiny teacher. May I continue to learn from you. Namaste.

SAVE THE DATE!

"Every time you tear a leaf off a calendar, you present a new place for new ideas and progress."

--Charles Kettering

Quick—what was the date of your son's first day of playgroup 25 years ago? When in 1993 did you go to the dentist? Do you know if 2000 was the year you went to the family reunion in Virginia?

Didn't think so.

Ah, but I know these dates in my life. You see, I took notes.

For a period of almost 30 years, I wrote the details of our comings and goings in those little datebooks Hallmark tucks into the bag when you buy greeting cards. There wasn't room to write much for each day, but I hit the highlights. As a result, I can look up almost any Sunday-Saturday from 1974-2002 and tell you (if you care) what my family and I were up to. I kept these records religiously for so long that it is a real pity I gave up.

After the Hallmark era, I had begun my job at church, and bought those annual day planners. These entries reflected only my professional life, but still they were useful for recalling specific moments in time. I can flip through and bring my fun-filled trip to the Lutheran synod assembly in '06 right back. Not that I necessarily want to, mind you...

We still keep a wall calendar in the kitchen, but these notations are spotty at best (PJ 3-5 w/ Z, Rose Dr. L. 2:40, buy coffee!!) and sometimes whole months go by and no one writes anything down. These are the months when we miss the birthday parties and book club meetings, because no one in the house can remember that well. Every year at this time, as Fall arrives and school and Steve's new theatre season and the church program year all start, I renew my vow to do better, but since 2003 we've gone pretty much un-chronicled.

A few months ago I was up in the attic and came upon a set of journals I wrote when Steve and I were on the road on our first children's theatre tour of the Northeast (beginning in Ticonderoga, NY in January of 1979). The days were busy indeed, but the nights afforded enough time for me to scribble the tales of our shows and travels in minute detail. Alas, this stint in our lives, scintillating to us as it was at the time, would never crack *The New York Times* bestseller list.

When floods and fires and tornadoes strike, I watch TV footage of families who have lost everything, including their scrapbooks, diaries and calendars. The keenest memory cannot begin to recapture the full story of them. This is why you see folks sifting through the ruins desperately for any trace of their history, and why it is such a sad and poignant sight.

Unless we prove to be famous in some way, few will value our dates and times and places in the future. So why bother?

Because it does matter. My time here matters to me. And I need some prompting to keep it all in mind. My life, every second of it, is a precious gift from God. It would be a sin (literally) to let it pass without even noticing, without somehow recording at least some details. A few well-chosen words can bring back an entire season of my earthly span. Sure, it takes a little effort to write things down. Sure, I'm busy. But am I really too busy to mark my days before they slip away?

So that settles it. I'm going back to Hallmark soon. The 2014 calendars will be coming out. 2014 will, I'm sure, bring new people, places and experiences into my life. I'm looking forward to it all. And later, I'll enjoy reliving those times prompted by my notes, thankful for the priceless opportunity to be on this amazing planet, living a life I cherish, for another year.